I Remember Union
The Story of Mary Magdalena

Dedicated

to

The Counsel

and

The Ones With No Names

I acknowledge:

Mary Magdalena, the Hierarchy of Order, Celandra,
the Mother Earth, the Fiber of Being, the Devic kingdom, and the Angels

Jayn Adina, my dear friend, whose patience, love and belief in
my vision of Mary made this book possible

My Mother, for always seeing me as I am

My Father, for your faith in me and the steadfastness of your love and guidance

My daughter, Debbie, for loving so much

My son, Jeff, for the joyfulness of your life

Grammy and Granddad for the examples you gave to me

Jim and Ivo for being my brothers

The Calhoun Family for our time together and the learning we accomplished

Noel McInnis for editing assistance and unwavering support of Mary

Peter Gerler, Lois Dean, and Deborah Cannarella for helping me to see
Mary more clearly

Patricia Hayes, Jan Hayes, Patricia St. John, Ann Phillips, and Susan Ericson
for teaching me about spirit

Carlee Janci for your friendship and help

Ann McGill for her concept of graphic writing

*All of you who have influenced, inspired and encouraged me,
contributing to my life and experience, I thank you.*

I give my special thanks to:

Nomad and Sheba, my constant and loyal four-legged friends,

whose love and companionship have never waivered

~~~

Robbie Gass, who first opened my heart

~~~

The memory of Squaw, the Golden Fish, and Saschai

The whales, the crows, the hawks, the eagles, and the dolphins

~~~

Lesley Waldron for being there

~~~

Those souls actively creating the model of Soul Recognition

in the world

~~~

The Heaven on Earth Community,

Adina, Albert, Carlee, Debbie, Gray Beaver, Hope, Jonathan, Martha,

Jeff and Marisa

for choosing to live the truth of union

Maundy Thursday
March 25, 1989
McLean, VA

An urgency filled me, an urgency I did not understand. I had planned to go to West Virginia with friends, but I was changing my mind. . . listening to a voice within me. A voice which said not to go, but to stay here and attend communion, the service in memory of The Last Supper.

I glanced at my watch, almost 8:30 PM. The service was probably half over. The night was cold and rainy. . . I hadn't been to church in a long, long time. I looked down at my hot pink bobby socks, sneakers, tight wool leggings, hot pink thigh-length sweater. Oh well, if I was going to do this, it was now or never. I asked my friends if they could help me find the nearest Presbyterian church. We got out the phone book and they gave me the directions. I said good-bye to my friends and ran to my car through the pouring rain.

I stood at the foot of the communion table, surrounded by twelve others. Outside, the rain poured relentlessly, mingling with the words of the service. The minister gave us the sacrament of holy communion, and I began to partake of the cup. I faced him as he stood at the head of the long table.

Suddenly, above his head I saw the shimmering figure of Jesus Christ! Hanging suspended in the air above the minister, He beckoned to me.

I stared at His image above me, iridescent, luminous, unworldly.
This light, the figure of Christ.
I looked around, unsure of what the figure wanted me to do. No one else appeared to see him, the ritual of sacrament proceeding as usual. I was awed, stunned. I felt out of place, as if I did not belong here.
Tears fell from my eyes, running down my cheeks. The people stared at me, aware of my tears.

As I received the bread and we finished partaking of the sacrament, we were told to return to our seats. The vision of Christ still before me, I turned, stumbling, to resume my seat as others filed to the table, 12 by 12.

I had seated myself in an empty pew at the edge of the congregation. Apart from the others, I closed my eyes to pray and to regain my composure. As I prayed, a scorching heat touched my forehead and hands. The heat intensified, burning me. I wanted to see where this heat was coming from, hoped to find a logical explanation. So I opened my eyes, looking up to see again, the shimmering figure of Christ.
He came closer and closer, and I waited and watched, holding my breath. What was happening? Why was He here? What did He want?

Then, with a wh-o-o-shing sound, He came toward me and then into me, merging with my upper body.
Suddenly an uncontrollable urgency filled me, an expansion, a radiance. I felt light-headed and confused, emotional and ecstatic, one part of me rejoicing, and one part of me questioning.

As we stood to sing the final hymn I tried to sing with the people, but I was suddenly afraid of them, afraid of their judgement, their watching me. I fled into the rainy night.

I ran to my car, jerked open the door and jumped in, the rain drenching me and the seat. I sat there, breathing heavily, tears streaming from within, trying to sort it all out.

And there before me on the windshield of my car, Christ appeared again! I was overwhelmed! Emotions raced through me: joy, fear, awe, embarrassment, a longing to understand and to merge, and a hesitancy to be seen. I felt different somehow—less rational, unclear, and yet, clearer than I had ever been before. Images crystallized before my eyes— memories of my search for answers about life, my yearning to find the meaning of existence, my commitment to spirit and truth.

Christ began to speak to me then, through my awareness. His thoughts communicated themselves to me without language.
He told me of Mary Magdalena and their love.
He imparted to me the essence of His life, and I listened. . . .

Later that same night the visions began. . . the visions of Christ and Mary Magdalena. They came to me powerfully and with immense clarity, the first one depicting their walk in the desert to the Sermon on the Mount. . . .

Four months later I began to record them.

The visions showed me the time of Christ through the eyes and perspective of Mary of Migdala, called Mary Magdalena.

They showed her and Christ as humans who remembered their oneness with all things and lived accordingly. I was shown the plan, the design to which they were both called and to which they gave their lives in service. I saw Mary and Jesus in Israel, France, Spain, India and Kashmir, and two months later I traveled to these countries in search of Mary. . . .

What I found, I knew was irrefutable. Mary was not a harlot, powerless, following Christ. She was a woman of extraordinary vision and power, facing her fears with immense courage and determination. Setting aside personal feelings and desires, she dedicated her life to upholding God and the greater design she had pledged to serve, regardless of the obstacles she encountered.

Her journey has inspired me, and her visions have expanded me.

She is a noble, beautiful, nurturing woman who will take you in her arms and call from you the memory and truth of who you are.

It has been the greatest gift of my life to know her.

Here is my story of Mary Magdalena. . . .

Shalom,

Flo Aeveia Magdalena

I REMEMBER UNION is the story of Mary Magdalena,
an endearing woman who remembers her oneness with spirit and with all
things. This memory guides her to the vision of peace, which she
endeavors to bring to the world.

With humility, courage, and compassion, she lives from her heart,
allowing no one else to shape her thinking or to influence the decisions of
her soul. She knows only she can decide her truth, and so with spunk and
determination she hones this truth as she lives, remembering the plan of
who she is, why she was born, and what she has come to do.
Sometimes she is judged, many times ostracized, but though she
experiences aloneness, fear, and separation, she continually chooses to
live the unity she remembers.

Resolutely she challenges the human laws which separate us from God,
each other, and the Earth.
She is dedicated to helping others remember their divinity, and assists
them to understand that if they remember, they will choose to live in
peace and unity.

Mary's story is the fulfillment of the promise of union.
As you read this book, I invite you to live this story with Mary,
feel her in your heart, and remember the magic of your soul,
the part of you that knows we are all one.

As you read Mary's story, remember union. . . .

Contents

INTRODUCTION

THE WORD

In the beginning was the word.
And the word was god.
And all was one.

And all of the knowledge of all time
was held within the core
of the source,
called god.

And there were no people.

The people were but a vision
of a time which had no dimension
and no form.

And god brought forth the vision,
and the people rose
to bring the word to the land
and to the generations of people
which would follow.

And so the journey into form began.

The form became separate from the vision
and from the source of the word,
called god.

With the separation fear was born.

And with the separation was the

breaking   apart

of the vision

into soul: male and female.

The separation created the need to reunite—

to return to the vision and to the source.

So the people traveled through time and space
to approach a land where the form could be used
to bring forth the link to the source
and to their essence, called "soul."

Planted into the memory of man and woman
was the knowledge of the source
called spirit,
called, in a word,

GOD.

God planted within the souls of men and women
a seed,
which housed the memory of their divinity
and of their birth into form.

And within the seed is the image of God,
and man and woman,
and all manner of life belonging to the same family,
and to the same soul,
and to the same way of the word.

And there was instilled a memory of a time

when all were one

and when all would be one again.

ALLWOULDBEONEAGAIN

When all is one,
there is a marriage of God
and man and woman
and the word
and the people
and the vision and the form
and the essence and the spirit.

And there is order created from this marriage
within and without,
which reflects the same reality,
and is called
"the truth."

As man and woman remember their calling,
the order becomes truth within them
and is known,
and so it is.

Now is the time for the **calling** to be remembered.

Now is the time for the **truth** to be remembered.

And in the remembering is the vision accomplished.

The form and the source are then one again.

And the journey is finished.

The vision and the form and the people and god are again

one.

Now is the time.

THE CHRYSTALLIS OF BEING

AS WE CHOOSE TO BECOME FORM
WE ENTER THE

CHRYSTALLIS OF BEING

the place of the soul's inception

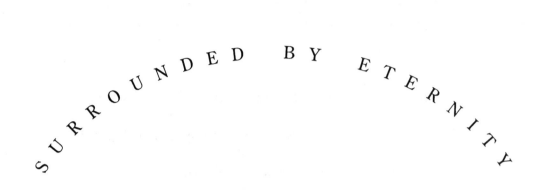

OUR SOUL IS BORN.

Then, one by one, the beings of light encircle us,

AS WE TRAVEL TO THE SWING BETWEEN WORLDS.

Here all of the knowledge of all time is known to us,

all is seen and remembered and realized.

As we choose our calling, our destiny, and our identity,

the beings of light speak to us about our journey.

They instruct us in the learning of our life lessons,
encouraging us to remember the design housed within.

Supported by these lights, we encode our calling

into the deepest aspect of our soul as a seed kernel

called **the seed of light,**

and we each remember this code

at exactly the chosen moment.

The beings of light and knowledge,
without faces, names or identities,
guide us and teach us
through love and patience,
so that we will remember
our soul's destiny.

And the ones with no names impart to us
that in the remembering will the soul's message
be brought into the world,
and the individual and collective destiny assured.

And that is how it begins.

THE SWING BETWEEN WORLDS

The Swing Between Worlds
Zero B.C.
Subject soul: Jesus Christ
Conversation before birth with The Nameless Ones

"It is the beginning," said The Nameless Ones.

"Yes," Jesus replied, "I know that this is true, and yet. . . ."

"And yet?" The Nameless Ones asked.

"I know that most of the people will think it is the end. It will take them, some of them, 2000 years to understand—to realize the truth. Many will think that I failed, and more importantly," he paused, "that you failed!"

"This distresses you?" they asked.

"Yes." Jesus paused, reflecting. "It seems so complex, so hard, in many ways, futile. Why are we creating this? So that the people will search again?" he asked.

They replied, "No, no. They have been searching long enough. It is now time for them to find—to recognize and to remember that they are no different from you. They truly know.

"The years of their learning are bringing them to the realization that they are one with you, as you are one with them. This is what they seek, the unity of all souls. You will love them enough to 'die' to prove that you are one with them. They will worship you for a time, until there is the consciousness to remember that the beginning and the ending are one, and that you and they are really the same."

Jesus asked, "Why do they always forget? Have they not had hundreds of examples? So many souls have shown them the light. We have done this so many times, in so many places, and in so many ways." He sighed. "You have so much patience, waiting for them to find their way home, more patience than I!"

The Nameless Ones explained,

"Did you not find your way? Was it not the same for you? Your consciousness has taken this 'time' to incorporate the learning and energy necessary to guide this process for 144 souls. Do you see the value in patience? We are now creating the most important pivotal soul span ever to be forged through time and planted in the Earth space. And you are one of the key figures upon which the other souls will spin.

These 144 souls will be born with you into the body of the Christ, and they will be called 'aspects.' They will merge to form the light which you will bring. And then, in 2000 years, when it is time for the light to be known and remembered on the Earth, the 'aspects' will be born again as individual souls.

"They will bring this light into being. The time will come for the
people to remember. They will know that they are the same as you
and have come to join with you to be the light."

"And remember," they said, "you will have Mary!"
Jesus asked, "Mary? Who is Mary?"

The Nameless Ones waited before replying.
"Remember, let yourself remember." They waited.

Jesus hesitated, "You mean," he asked, "I do not have to do this alone?
This Mary will be there with me? What does this mean? There are so
many questions! Who will she be? Is hers the energy I feel so strongly
now? Is she a part of me?"

When he received no answers, he paused and let the knowing
come to him, remembering that he had all the answers.

"Yes," he stated, "that is her energy and she is a part of me, a part of me
yet in another physical form!" he exclaimed.

He paused again, digesting this, as if he had to absorb it to fully let it in.
"She is me, isn't she?   She and I . . . Oh!"

He stopped, overcome with relief.
"I thought. . . I mean . . . man's records indicate. . . ."
He felt an enormous weight being lifted from him.

"We would not send you to do it alone," they replied.
"We are loving you too much."

Jesus felt this love and assurance, and suddenly all the
questions were answered.
There really is no aloneness anywhere—
no abandonment, no betrayal.

There   would   be   no   betrayal!

He sighed and immediately felt light flood his soul.

"See, now, what your learning will be," said The Nameless Ones gently.

Jesus, reflecting, hesitated ever so slightly, and began looking into the
Akashic records, where the evolution of the universe is recorded.
"To trust in the process of true creation;
to trust in you, and in myself, and in Mary;
to trust!"
He paused, catching his breath on his last words,
and then continued:
"To acknowledge you when man disdains you;
and to remember, to truly remember."

He continued:

> "I know, also, that I will live truth and order,
> even when there is no human example of it.
> I will live it even when I perceive
> I am far from your love and support and
> question your validity.
> I will still live it."

"The destiny you have chosen is to fulfill that learning, and it is so.
Rest assured," they said with love.

"Will we help the people to remember the unity of all souls?" he asked.

"Yes," they replied. "Ultimately, yes. The part you will play is necessary
and of monumental importance. You see, they need an example,
and you will give it to them."

Well contented, Jesus said, "I understand, and I am ready."

"Does your soul give permission for re-entry according to
the designed plan?" asked The Nameless Ones.

"Yes," said Jesus.

"Before you go, remember these truths:

> Remember that you are God.
> Remember that there is no time.
> Remember that we are loving you very much.
> Remember that you are never alone. Remember!"

They charged the air with the words, branding them into his consciousness, as if they could forge them into his awareness for all time.

Jesus felt the beings of light, and knew them. He drank them in, as if knowing that it would seem a long time before he would be with them again. He drew upon the moment, expanding it to encompass his whole being—all moments, all time, all experience. Finally, he nodded his readiness to proceed.

The Nameless Ones directed him to again look into the records.

"See now your destiny and the soul who is your female counterpart.
See her and begin to feel the divinity of your union,
for this is the pathway of your remembrance.
Allow her to draw you forward."

Jesus positioned himself in the Swing between Worlds, allowing his consciousness to flow into the place of records. He began seeing and experiencing the merging of time and space, the moments of future creation.

All was coming together in a moment of time.
All was in and of unity, and there was no separation.

He began to understand that this union was what he would
return to the Earth to teach and embody.

He felt again the familiar rush of wind, the return of
clarity, and the ability to see everything,

Past   Present   Future

and he became lost in the vision.

The Swing Between Worlds
Zero B.C.
Subject soul: Judas Iscariot
Conversation before birth with The Nameless Ones

And Judas said, "I will be the scapegoat—the darkest soul of all time!!"

"The people will learn the truth," said The Nameless Ones.

"Yes, but when? We know there is no time, but they do not know that. How long will it take them—2000 years? I am not sure about this at all!" said Judas.

"You have free will to choose another role. You do want to be there, do you not?" they asked.

"Yes, yes! Without hesitation, I can honestly say that I want to be there, and I do want to help him. He is as I, after all."

He paused and reflected for what seemed a long time.
"It has to be this way? This is the way it has to be?" he asked.

The Nameless Ones did not reply, waiting for him to see the design.

"Yes," he said, "all right." He added, more a statement than a question, "It has to be one who loves him more than life itself," he paused, "does it not?"

"Yes," they replied.

"It seems a hard thing—a cruel thing," he said. He contemplated for a long time, thinking about and experiencing all that would transpire if he made this choice. "I know that someone must do it. You are sure he will know that I have not betrayed him?" he asked, as an affirmation.

The Nameless Ones did not reply.
"Yes, I know. I can see it. I am holding it off," he admitted.
"Well, then, yes, I will do it. I will do it!" shouted Judas.
"I create it!"

He felt relief now that he had come to a decision.
Now that he had chosen.

There was a long pause as he pondered it all.

"When I do this, I can see I am going to be alone—alone for a very long time. I will have no one—no one." He paused again to look into the records. "There will be no one. I will be completely alone."

He paused once more, and then blurted out, "This is a great opportunity! Do you realize what I will accomplish?" He looked at The Nameless Ones and felt their joy at his discovery.

He breathed deeply into his soul and a glow formed around him.
"This will bring me what I have searched for, throughout eternity!"
He began dancing joyfully in the Swing.

"What is that?" they asked.

Judas answered excitedly, "I will find myself. I will find myself!"

"Yes," they said.

Judas continued, "There will be no one else.
When he is gone, I will have to find myself—"

"Yes," they responded, "and in so doing, find him again."

Judas gathered himself together and said, "I am ready."

"Does your soul give permission for re-entry according to the
designed plan?" they asked.

"Yes," he answered.

The Nameless Ones instructed him,

> "Remember that you are a part of the divine plan.
> Remember that the 'illusion' of the world
> is not the truth;
> Remember that you are trusted beyond
> measure—Remember!"

They paused and then said, "Look again into the records and
we will begin."

Judas drew a deep breath of life into his soul and began focusing on the
records. He was excited and afraid, and yet the meaning was very clear to
him—the true meaning.

And he was at peace.

The Swing Between Worlds
Zero B.C.
Subject Soul: Mary Magdalena
Conversation before birth with The Nameless Ones

Mary Magdalena said, "They will think I am a whore!"

"It is all a matter of perspective," replied The Nameless Ones.

Mary repeated, "They will think I am a whore!"

"It is only a matter of perspective," they answered.

"Is there no other way?" she asked.

"Why are you so grieved?" they asked.

"I will be judged," she said.

"We understand," they said.

"I will be judged," she said again, and her heart and soul cried out.

The Nameless Ones enfolded her in light, and she grew calmer.

"Then what is your learning to be?" they asked.

She pondered, just as the counterparts of her soul were doing in parallel experiences in the Swing between Worlds.

> "To have faith in divine justice
> and to know and remember my mission."

She paused.

"To have faith in divine justice," she repeated, as if understanding it for the first time. "If I do that," she said, "I will be free, will I not?"

There was a long silence.

"Yes," they said.

"What a relief," she said. "To have faith in it, finally," she ended, feeling gratitude and resolution.

"There is more learning," they reminded her.

"Yes, I know." She answered almost stubbornly, for she loved them and knew the records, and was not yet ready to leave.

> "I see that I will inspire Jesus
> to his greatest potential, and that
> I must appear less important
> and less powerful because the
> age of Pisces is created for men
> to be dominant in the world."

And because the thought was distasteful to her, she sighed and then said,
                    "I will learn to be humble."

They waited as she accepted this and came to peace with it, and
then they said, "You seem perplexed."

Mary answered, "Yes, it is intricate, is it not? Nothing that appears true
on the surface will be the truth. So how will the people come to know the
truth and integrate the understanding?"

"Ah!" they answered. "That is the beauty of the design!
Remember that when they allow the light within them
to shine, all time will become one moment,
and all will be again in unity.
The truth will stand.
They   will   see
and it will all come together:

THE   HOLOGRAM   OF   TRUTH!

They will see you as you truly are!"

Mary asked, "Will they see you also? Will they come to see
you and know you as I do?"

"Yes," they answered very gently, "why else do you go?"

She felt their love and support, and smiled. She answered, "I do understand, yet I feel their judgement so strongly within me. And for him, too. I can feel him exploring in my consciousness and merging with the crystals of light within me."

"It is very beautiful, is it not?" they answered. "He has been searching for you for a long time. You see, you are the answer to the question, the piece of the puzzle. He is nothing without you, as you are nothing without him. For you are the same and have always been the same.

Male and female—You are one.

He has traveled the universe looking for you, and now he will find you. And the magic will draw many to you to experience the union— the union of souls."

They paused. "It is time," they said.

"Yes," she answered, gathering the forces of light around her.

"Does your soul give permission for re-entry according to the designed plan?" they asked.

"Yes," she said.

"We will now discuss the design with you further. Set your vision on the Swing, and join him as you create the 'reality' of the resurrection together.

"And always remember these things, my dear:

>Remember you have free will.
>Remember you are light and so you shall remain.
>Remember there is no right or wrong,
>only divine truth;
>Remember that if you ask, you shall receive.
>Remember!"

She nodded, and breathed in the light of the truth of being and merged her consciousness with the male part of her soul, the one who would be called Jesus Christ.

She began to travel through time and space, losing all except
> the   truth   of   the   order   of   being.

>It had begun.

THE BIRTHS

They each felt the tunnel,

a   whirling   pattern   of   fast-flowing,

counterclockwise energy

pushing them   forward   into the abyss.

They knew they were safe,   and yet   the pressure   was

crowding their consciousness,   and they were unsettled.

The vibrations   were increasing   in concentric

circles   and yet   becoming   more dense

at the same time.

They tried to remember their instructions

and to be clear in their design.

They traveled faster and faster down the tunnel,

the canal of birth, each moving into the body

which would house the soul

and its encoded instructions for its chosen work.

They seemed lost as the speed increased

and they were no longer sure of their direction.

Their eyes were full

of the v i s i o n s of a l l time,

and they knew not their true identities,

only the ones they had chosen

for this life perception.

They would each arrive at their chosen destination
with the parents and life experience
they had designed in the Swing.

And they would be

s e p a r a t e

for a time
from spirit
and from each other,

as they adjusted,
choosing how much of their parents'
belief system
they would accept as their own.

The times were approaching when they would arrive,

and the speed increased.

The velocity and the vibration

increased in a way that they had almost

forgotten:

THE VIBRATION OF ILLUSION.

Pattern after pattern of fear
and judgement
would be fed over and over again to the arriving souls.

The arrival was inducing a t e m p o r a r y a m n e s i a.

"Where am I?   Who am I?   Why have I come?"

And as they lost the truth,

they h e l d to the

LIGHT

as they traveled,

F O R   T H E R E   W A S   N O T H I N G   E L S E.

Because they were of the Hierarchy of Order
they would remember more than most,
and because of the design they would resist less.

And so it was assured.

Within them their consciousness forged with form,

merging the four levels—spirit, mind, emotion, and body—

and they

BECAME   HUMAN.

They sighed:

THEY   HAD   ARRIVED.

MY FIRST TURNING

MY BIRTH

I, Mary Magdalena, was the first to enter,

for I had come to prepare the way for the others.

I was held in transition for a shorter time,
and therefore remembered more of the design.

I began to invoke the Goddess,
for her gifts were necessary for me
as a female child
to stay grounded through time and space
and be affected by neither.

I repeated, as I had been instructed:

I am spirit
and spirit I shall remain always
unaffected by human laws and
interpretations of truth.

And the boldness of the design came upon me,
and I was afraid.

I was living in many realities;
and the design was to bring
the truth of unity
into the twenty-first century.

Bold, perhaps unbelievable.

Those of Christ's time were in search of the outer God,
did not understand the implications of God,
were not prepared to house God within them.

If they knew that God was within
they would run from their own shadows
and hide from their own souls in fear.

Not yet—not until the learning was accomplished,
not for 2000 years.
And yet, I could see myself in that life also
and in all the lives in between.

MY CHILDHOOD

My bond with my mother was pure and strong. Of the lineage of Isis, she remembered her heritage from the Goddess, and in her heart was the dedication of light. She knew her purpose and was committed to it without question. She had come to teach and to heal, and I had chosen to be with her, for she could guide me in my unfolding and in the merging of my spirit and soul into my body.

We dreamt and visioned together each day. She assured me that I was spirit and reminded me of the truth and of the design. Each day she affirmed my light and guided this light through the bottoms of my feet. Holding me to her heart and rocking me, she wove the sound of the beating of her love into the beating of my heart, so I would know it there always.

She told me of the Swing between Worlds and reminded me of my calling, pledging with her heart and intention to walk beside me always.

Her eyes were dark, starlit—their light full with remembrance, dignity, and knowledge. They followed me, even when she could not see me, and I knew her presence always.

She taught me to merge with nature and the kingdoms and, through ritual, guided me to remember the cycles and rhythms of life. We celebrated the sun's rising and setting each day and the moon's rising each night, holding ceremonies on the full moon and at the turning of the seasons.

She helped me listen to the sounds of the Earth—the wind and the stars, the birds and the creatures—which guided me in balancing my cells in order with the fluids of the universe.

She sat with me, undemanding, allowing me to grow as I chose, honoring my truth. She knew the natural cadence of my unfolding as if it were her own and gave it sanction.

Her God was as real to her as I, and she acted accordingly. She saw only the good, projected only perfection, and therefore, realized it. Those who saw her never forgot her. She would draw her presence forth and merge with their souls, and they would feel therefore refreshed.

The most valued gift I received from her was her choice never to judge me. It was the first place in the world where I was not judged.

When I would question or falter, she would reach with her eyes and her presence and find me in my doubt and darkness and draw me out—draw my essence forth so I felt it again. She knew the way of the path of service well and gave her full attention to helping me find my direction there.

I was her favorite, for we were of the same soul seed, and my destiny to bring all souls home was hers as well. We felt a great comfort and satisfaction in the unfolding of our destiny, knowing we shared it together.

We talked without words, even after I learned to speak with the tongue. Our communion was clear, direct, and from the heart.

I questioned everything, and she explained to me in pictures, teaching me to see without my physical eyes and to hear without my physical ears.

I was initiated into the sisterhood of the Goddess on my twelfth birth day, at the time of my blooming. My mother and the mother of Jesus, and the sisterhood of the village, all over their twelfth year, took me to the sacred cave of darkness and taught me their ways.

I learned of the healing crystals, the elements and minerals of the Earth, the wands of magic, and the importance of sharing rituals with other women. I pledged a bond never to betray a woman, another sister, in all the days of my living.

At my initiation we honored the moon and danced in the night, and I learned how to bond through my feet to the Earth and to open my feminine pathway to receive substance. They opened me to draw upon this feminine substance so I could create in the world.

They told me that when I fully experienced my female energy, the substance of the universe would be there for me to create anything that I would need and that this substance is innately understood by women because they are here to procreate.

I was taken into the sacred circle and they taught me, through visions, about mating: touching my body and awakening my memory of passion and giving me permission to love, to nourish my essence, and to have pleasure through my body.

I learned that men and women instinctively mate to merge the *knowledge* of the male God with the *creation* of the female Goddess. Their offspring are then in balance, the male and the female within each child blending in harmony. If the parents understand their role, they and their children then live in union within themselves, in their families, and in the world, creating the balance of order through love and trust.

The women of the cave of darkness were wise, and I loved and respected them very much. In the early years of my growing, however, I had wondered if I was different from them in some way, and after my initiation, I knew it was so.

In the cave of darkness the women were joyful, powerful, and wise. In the world outside the cave, however, they were solemn and still, masterful only in their rituals and with each other, and not with the men. I observed this also in my mother.

I, though, was learning to maintain my presence wherever I was. I did not bow down to the temple or the elders or the rabbis. I bowed only to the Gods. I respected others, but did not allow them to force me to act in a way which was not consistent with my truth.

As I grew older, I was aware of two different truths or realities; the truth I had learned in the Swing Between Worlds—the knowing that we are all one, and the truth I had learned in the world—the illusion that we are separate and alone.

Knowing this difference, I assumed others knew it also. And then I learned that they did not remember the Swing and thus were afraid— afraid to speak, afraid to choose a new road, afraid to dream, and afraid to live.

At first I was aghast, and then sad, and then resigned. And then I realized that I was here to help change this and did not need to conform. And so I was free again—free except with my father, my earthly father.

He had forgotten the truth of oneness, even as he professed to remember it, walking the path of the cloth—the path of the rabbi. His beliefs overshadowed his knowing, and he confused his beliefs with the truth. He was intelligent, firm, and just. Attached to the tradition of the people, he believed that it was his duty to uphold it.

As he watched me begin my healing work, he challenged my ways, saying that only God could heal—only God knew the way of the miracle. I told him that when we remember our soul and our oneness with all things there is no pain and dis-ease, and that was what I was teaching the people.

He told me that pain was a teacher—it was the way that God taught us. I told him that God did not create our pain, but he would not listen. He would say to me, "No—no, no—no, no—" And the discussion would end.

My beliefs defied his logic, and as I stridently affirmed my essence, he saw me living without fear of God, and he grew more and more confused.

My boldness shocked him.

He thought me irreverent. He could not understand me, and he became distant as he weighed my beliefs against his own.

It was not that he did not love me. It was the opposite.
His immense love choked him. He knew I would be cast out. And, so, he cast me out himself, as if he could prepare me by facing me with his judgement first. For this was the tradition—if a woman did not obey the law, she was judged harshly by the people.

For him, the law was the pathway to God.
For me, the soul was the pathway to God.

And because our beliefs were different, he kept me from his heart, and so we stayed apart.

THE VOID

To feel as if you do not belong
anywhere
is a special kind of
a l o n e n e s s.

It leaves an imprint of emptiness within,
perhaps a void.
And there is nowhere to turn.
And that is how I felt.

Sometimes, with someone I loved,
there was a place to reside,
a place to rest, to merge,
and to become
o n e
in the way of all.

And then, there would be this
return of aloneness
when they were gone
that would shatter the sense
of oneness
and lead me back to
despair
and to no-thingness.

Deep in my self, I would weep,
yearning for my soul to reveal itself
more plainly as my friend,
so I could embrace it and call it to me,
and know again the truth of my unity
with all things.

And it would not come.

Like a recalcitrant child,
my soul would linger
within the far reaches of my being
when I would call.

DOES THE SOUL BELONG TO US OR DOES IT NOT?

Where is the design that we cannot find it at each moment
and in each yearning ?

I reached inside and called,

and it did not come.

And

I SCREAMED INTO THE VOID—

a silent scream—

and cursed my existence

and the design

and the plan that led me

to such a point of aloneness.

AND I WAS ALONE.

I was exhausted,
    and I rested
        in the only place I knew—
            in that void
                within that aloneness.

        It carried me
            and I went,
                unresisting.

            It carried me,
                and I went.
                    We traveled,
                        and I let go and surrendered,
                            and I went.

        I began to feel no-thingness around me,
            the place of the void,

ENCLOSING ME AND SURROUNDING ME,

and ultimately   to my surprise,

    s u p p o r t i n g   m e.

I relaxed into the place of no-thing

    I   G R E W   A N D

          I   E X P A N D E D.

I allowed myself to not define my safety,
               and I felt safe.

I allowed myself to be alone
               and to stay there.

When I would resist,
and try to return to the place of human despair,
I would feel the emptiness there,
and the void felt richer,

           more alive,

           and I would go again, within.

And I let go even more,
allowing the moment to be whatever it was.

Thoughts would enter about all manner of things
to distract me from the moment,
and I would return within,
knowing that there was no place else to go,
nowhere that was more safe.

I would bargain with the no-thing space within,
but it was not fooled.
There was no escape except to be there.
No one who would rescue me from this search.

So I went inward and became stronger.
I followed the path of my soul
into the bowels of my creation.

And suddenly I felt   l i g h t   returning to my mind,
as if the light was emanating from deep within me,

and it was!

I opened to receive it, and it shone upon me
the way a child joyfully
welcomes one back from a long journey.

There was a child inside there,
and discovery,
and joy!
And all the things which I had sought outside myself!

There was a pulsing and a deepening—
an invitation,

and I accepted.

I went forward
catching my breath,
and the welcome remained.
There was no withdrawal
as I went nearer.

I expanded more, reaching within,
and rather than less,
there   was   m o r e

a n d   m o r e

A N D   M O R E.

I did not end,

I was not hollow,

I was not empty.

I was f u l l

and F U L L E R.

THE JOURNEY HOME HAD BEGUN.

THE SEA OF GALILEE

The Sea of Galilee was the place where I went to learn of my heritage from God and the Goddess and practiced working with the laws and levels of the force fields of nature.

A few months after my initiation into the sisterhood of the Goddess, my mother came to me and said that the Mother Mary had invited us to go with her and Jesus and his cousin Elisabeth to the Sea of Galilee. The Mother asked me to accompany them because I was now a woman, and it was time for me to learn and to foster my calling. We would spend many months in the north country, learning and practicing together.

And so a week later, my mother and I gathered our robes and sleeping cloths, jugs for water and pots for cooking, and set out early in the morning. We made our way slowly, savoring the time alone together. My sister and brother remained in Migdala with my aunt and my father, which bespoke the importance of this journey. My mother had spoken with my father, telling him she must sojourn with me to the Sea to teach me the ways of my calling. It was the first time she was forceful with him, overcoming his resistance, listening not to his objections.

We reached the north shore of the Sea at the time of the supping, where the Mother and Jesus and Elisabeth awaited us. We were all very excited to be there, sharing in the preparations of our first meal together.

After supping, we had ritual: the Mother Mary placed us each in the position of the four directions—my mother to the north, Elisabeth to the west, Jesus to the east, and I to the south. She spoke to the directions, calling them to assist us in our ceremony. She called to the Mother Earth and the Father Sky, the Grandmother and the Grandfather, and all of the lights, the devas, and the angels and asked for their presence during the days and weeks of our time there. She claimed her divine right to know the records of our unfoldment and to assist us in the process of anchoring light and knowledge into our consciousness.

She sanctified our learning and called in the dimensions to assist us. The Mother told us of the Mother Earth's calling, and we made an agreement with the elements and the kingdoms to guide our learning. She spoke these words to us as we sat under the stars:

> The Earth is our Mother. At the beginning of Earth time she chose to foster the learning of the people about their free will, assisting us in our journey to oneness. She pledged her support and nurturance to make our learning possible, knowing that this was the fulfillment of her highest destiny. She took an oath to remain constant and to allow the people free will to choose their actions and their destinies, regardless of the consequences to her. She chose to maintain a constancy which is experienced in the laws of gravity and matter.

> The pathway of power that we are learning is that of communication and awareness of the Earth's levels of consciousness so that they are available to us, and so that we can affect the laws of matter.

We enact these rituals to honor the Earth and her decision to help us return to oneness.

She is a living organism with consciousness, and her kingdoms— the plants, the animals and the minerals—communicate to keep the balance of nature in order. She receives substance from the invisible, from the ethers or spiritual level of her body, just as we do, and can assist us in gathering this substance to us. This is the manna or essence of the universe.

As she blooms, we bloom; as she has unlimited abundance, so do we; as she creates, we create; as all of her species and kingdoms live in balance and harmony from her guidance, so do we, in choosing to live from our essence—the essence which binds us to all life.

The pathway of power is created from the memory that there is no separation between the invisible and the visible—between substance and form. Those who retain this memory know that there is no separation between the spheres or the kingdoms and live within all the levels of consciousness. They experience no limitation. They can transcend the human belief in time and space, and looking into the Akashic records, can see all time: they know that they are one with the Gods and all kingdoms.

Oneness is created from this pathway. When the force of life is not tempered by the mind, it is available for the essence and the soul.

When oneness is the experience, there is a bonding between the will and matter. The atoms and molecules of the Earth's substance then accord the will. In this way it is possible to materialize and dematerialize matter. The frequency of the cells matches the molecules of the kingdoms, and they are unified.

The water of the Sea of Galilee has special properties: the molecules expand and contract according to the will. The water has made a pact with the Gods to foster our learning and to encourage our calling, and so we have come here to the Sea to learn of this.

When you speak to the water through your thoughts, it will adjust its form to accommodate you.

Remember that the laws and levels of the Earth are sacred, and
your will must be attuned to the highest good of all concerned, or
your instruction will not be accorded.

Later, as I wrapped myself in warm cloths and lay down under the stars,
I thought of this evening and the specialness of our first supping together,
and the sacredness of the ritual the Mother had spoken for us. And I
remembered her words as if she had scribed them in my mind. I felt
proudly the knowing of my calling and spoke a silent vow of love to the
Earth before I slept.

The next afternoon, Elisabeth and I sat on the rocks by the sea, talking
about our lives and our future. She was my dearest friend, two years older
than I. Her mother, the sister of the Mother Mary, had died when
Elisabeth was small, and Mary then raised Elisabeth and her sister
Miriamne. They both spent much time with Jesus, helping to care for him,
calling him brother.

As we sat by the sea dipping our feet in the water, we spoke of all manner
of things. In the ways of women, we spoke words about life and the design,
and of how we would teach those who would lead the people. We spoke of
men and what it was to be women in the world, of the act of human
merging, of our deepest feelings, and of our greatest dreams and desires.

We could sense the water listening to us and according us. It began to
speak to us through our senses about the elements and the kingdoms,
and we came to love and trust it as a friend.

It taught us how to hear the voice of the wind in the trees and to understand its cadence, and how to walk the earth and listen to her voice through our feet.

Then, many days later, the water called us to merge with it, and we began to practice walking on the sea. We felt no fear, for the water was our friend, and we listened to its instruction.

It told us that there would come a time when Jesus would use this pact to show the people the power of the pathway, and so we must remember this pathway and teach it to him.

To remember, we talked to the elements and reached deep within us to the past of all time to bring forth the knowledge which we sought.

When we were first learning, our mothers guided us, helping us to effect the connection with the realms of being. We had many days when we would all sit and play images across our consciousness, seeing the past and the future touching the moment, simultaneously. The moment would expand into years, and yet stay defined, reintegrating slowly and clearly. This experience allowed us to see all time in one moment.

We would then know the outcome when we knew the beginning, and so use our perception to see the choices which were possible for us to create. There was no limitation in the experience. Seeing everything, we had the ability to effect whatever was necessary to fulfill the design.

This brought time and space together and we created outside of time. We saw all realities and all possibilities, and were not limited by the laws of man.

We knew that our mothers were transferring to us the power of the shaman—the pathway of being. I would transfer this power to Jesus, and Elisabeth would assist me.

She and I had chosen to work closely together as had our mothers before us, helping and supporting each other. When we viewed the future we saw that we would be together for many years preparing for our most important work, which would be at the time of the resurrection.

The records showed us that at the moment of the crucifixion, Elisabeth would be on one side of Christ and I on the other, hidden at a distance in the trees, holding his consciousness between us in the realms of being, between this place of earth and the place of the Hierarchy, called heaven.

She and I would keep him alive in these stages of transition so that he could come again into form and finish his work here.

We practiced diligently, knowing it would take all of the twenty-five years between for us to perfect it. Elisabeth and I explored the other fully, knowing each other as we knew ourselves, for it was necessary to assure the outcome. We spoke of our fears and felt them in our bodies and guided each other to release them. We talked of aloneness and separation and shared our experiences, one to the other. I told her that sometimes when I was alone at night—

I felt the moments of aloneness
as points of an arrow—
that if I moved into aloneness,
the pain would become   d i s p e r s e d
and cease to be,
allowing me to merge
with my full consciousness.

I chose at times to believe in aloneness
and not reach out into the void.
I would resist my knowing
and call to me the forces of darkness and fear
and stay in the pain of the human
and believe I was alone.

It was an old place, familiar,
and I longed to be free of it,
longed to be full of the knowing
that I was still one with God.

Elisabeth knew of what I spoke and so we practiced reaching into the void together, dispersing the aloneness through our joining. We attuned our bodies, our minds, and our souls, learning to create oneness through our intent.

We talked of our hopes, our expectations, and our purposes, and helped each other to actualize them. We would match our breathing, our heart rate, and our consciousness. We practiced this first together, and then from great distances, to assure that we would know the other's state of being at all times.

We stayed in this space of limitlessness as much as we could, knowing ultimately that this was the place of our full power and calling.

Sometimes, even though we had each other and knew the design, we would forget this potential and see only the actual: the limits and laws of man. And when this would happen, we asked to remember the reason we had come and breathed again into the space of simultaneous reality.

We watched the Mother turn water into wine and multiply the numbers of fish and fowl to feed us. And as we remembered our knowing, we walked on water and practiced manifesting from substance as she did, acknowledging our need and calling forth the results to fulfill that need.

We unified more and more with spirit, opening the cells of our bodies and merging with the fiber of being—the thread which binds all life. We communicated with all species and listened to their language of light, clarifying our mission to live peacefully here with all forms of life.

We used all of our resources in each moment, and our ability to heal intensified as we each acknowledged our part in the design, learning to bond with each other, to merge our spirits, and to love unconditionally. We all unified our knowledge more and more with the experience of our being, learning to live the pathway we had chosen.

And for each of us, this choice was a beautiful one, for it began the fulfillment of our callings.

AND THEY CAME TO ME, THE PEOPLE

My hair was colored with henna, its highlights red-gold in
the sunlight, upon the black.

In my cells was the m a g i c of the night
and as I walked,
the moon and the essence of the Goddess
p u l s e d from my body.

A rhythm vibrated
as s h i m m e r i n g s t a r l i g h t on water,
barely perceptible, an illusion of movement
overlying density,
and it e x c i t e d the senses.

My spirit merged
with the cells of my body
and there was a dance
as they spoke, one to the other,
as wind and fire uniting
e x p l o s i v e
to fuel the fullness
of my expression in being.

A r a d i a n c e surrounded me,
an aliveness
permeated the air
and set me apart.

The people felt this radiance
and were drawn to it, and therefore to me.

They came expecting me to give them something—
physical pleasure, love, soothing.
They would leave not knowing what I had done,
and yet knowing at the same time.

It was different from anything they had
experienced before: form, and yet,   f o r m l e s s.

They would expect me to do what their wives,
husbands, mothers, fathers, lovers, or friends had done,
and I would not.
For my calling was to their soul,
and I served it as my master
and would not stray from my calling.

They   came   to   learn   of   their   immortality,
the   true   lessons   of   the   soul,
for there was nowhere else for them to learn it.
Their religion taught them only what they were not:
took from them their power,
did not reflect to them the truth of their own divinity.
It was incredible that they believed this judgement came
from the creator of life.

God would not act as such.

They would yearn to understand their soul's calling,
to listen to the code of the destiny within them,
and they would learn of me
and find their way to my door.

They came, for I lifted up their hearts,
their souls, their bodies, and their spirits,
nurturing their essence
so they felt and knew
their power and their purpose again.

They came to me in the night and the day
for the experience of

T h e   I n i t i a t i o n   I n t o   B e i n g.

It would take many forms, this journey.
Fear had locked them into the prison of their minds,
and together we would free them.
Rather than fearing God or death or separation,
they learned to honor themselves
and to know the purpose of their choice to be human.
They learned to face the fear of the void within them,
the darkness which they had come to name as
sin, vulgarity, hatred and vengeance.

At first, as the void called them to its brink,
they would stumble and hold back in terror.

And then they chose to find themselves—
coming to the void
having the courage
to leap from the world of i l l u s i o n and f e a r
and fly with wings unseen,
trusting the invisible.

To be with the people in this way
was my greatest calling.
It was for me a gift,
the same as being home,
a blessing from the Gods.

Their bodies were the entry into their soul,
the path of their divinity,
and I would touch them in the centers of their energy
as a gentle healer.

They had forgotten that
when the awareness directs the pathway,
the frequencies of the
body, emotion, mind, and spirit
are balanced.

They had been taught to direct their pathway with their mind,
and so their frequencies were unbalanced,
causing separation, fear, and dis-ease
in the body, and so they would come to me.

I would call forth the life within them,
banishing the fear
and bringing about a merging of these levels
into unity, balancing the frequencies.

I breathed the current
of the fiber of being into their cells
as I had been taught.
I called forth from them
their l i g h t and l i f e.
The cells knew who I was and
d a n c e d within the framework
of   their   universe
and laughed in remembrance
of their true being.

They would sleep as I made the sounds
of the angels' flutes into their cells,
and the levels would come into harmony.
When they awoke,
a fine mist of sweat covered their flesh
from what had been released
and a glow of warm red
appeared in their cheeks.
They felt as if the Gods
had d a n c e d in their hearts,
as of course
they had.

Coming to see me again,
I would anchor light
into the darkness
which they held as beliefs
within the physical body.

Again through my breath
I would touch them gently
in the places of their power
creating a wave of energy.

Their life force then rose within their spines.
They felt the joy and excitement of freedom
and the acknowledgment of belonging,
trusting the body with their spirit.
The body would come alive and dance.
This would sometimes feel
like a physical release, or
a sexual release,
but it was not.

They diminished their force of life
by living from their minds,
and so their only experience of this life force
was through the sexual act.

They wondered how this wave of life
could be fostered and nurtured,
experienced within their cells and levels
and in their lives.
And when they came back to me,
I would show them this.

I taught them to create aliveness
by balancing their male and female,
their human and divine,
their knowledge with substance.

They came to feel this unity
within themselves,
and to share this with another soul
who did not judge them.

Our bond reached through
the human vale of tears
transcending our bodies
and our identities.
For a time
they remembered their origin
and their divinity.

They talked of it in different words
but it was always the same,
the merging into **oneness,**

the remembrance of the fiber of being.

As they remembered their union with all,
we lived the reality of union together.

And because it was
the nearest thing to home,
it fed me continually with truth
in an untrue world.

And therefore,

I   R E J O I C E D

THE SHIELD OF PROTECTION

I saw only their souls, for how else could I do
what I had come to do?

For what else matters but the soul?

There are many ways to bring light to man and to woman, and
I knew them all. I was committed to helping them realize
the light, for all that mattered was that they remember it.

I had seen that when they do not remember, there is
killing and stealing and raping, and the judgement.
Oh, the judgement! The illusion of the world is judgement,
duality, dichotomy, and it cut me like a knife over and over again.

And so I created a shield, invisible to the naked eye,
to defend myself against the judgement.
At first it was unconscious, and then it was reinforced
as I spent more and more days
in the world of illusion.

Then, one night, the messenger of the angels came to me, saying:

> "Take ye from within the shield of protection,
>   for it serveth not thee."

I shrank back, pretending not to understand.

And the angel spoke again:

> "Since ye has come to learn the lesson of
>   divine judgement, ye must allow the lesson
>   to be learned."

The angel did not wait for a reply, but began to show me the
visions of the difference between

protection   and   resolution.

The angel showed me the outcome of each choice, and I was made aware.

> I saw that I would be alone if the protection
>   was stronger than the loving.

> If I feared others
>   or the outcome,
>   did not allow them into my heart,
> I would not succeed in my mission, for
>   the resolution of judgement is love.
> I must be present in the moment
>   for the love to transcend the fear.

I could love only if I was vulnerable.

And also, perhaps more importantly, if I stayed in the
love, always with the love, in each of those moments the
love would guide me home and fill my soul,
and hold up for them to see
the image of their own perfection.

Their judgement would fade as they felt the love,
and we would be joined outside the walls of fear,
remembering our oneness.

And so I chose to love and therefore resolved
to shatter my shield of protection.

I breathed into the shield and sent it
crashing, psychically and physically, into the
fortresses of God called the mountains.

And the mountains received the shield and tore it asunder,
taking the atoms from which it was made,
and removing the images, real and unreal,
of the fear and separation,
intentionally infusing

l i g h t

into the dark.

And when it was done,
and the Gods had received my decision,
they rejoiced.

For I now joined them
in t h e v i s i o n of t r u t h.

I no longer chose protection,
for loving filled me and freed me
from the duality of believing
that we are separate, or need protection.

And I remembered that they were I, and I was they,
and we were one.

And it was a blessing.

THE LIGHT OF MY CALLING

The dream was complete.
I was light.
There was nowhere that I was not,
for I was light.

Each cell opened to expand its dimension.
Light had dominion over my body,
and the cells acquiesced.

The light was the code of the life within me.
My senses responded
by allowing the light to direct the flow of awareness.
And the light did so,
suggesting the harmony to each atom
and calling forth its perfection.

My cells danced,
agreeing to be ordered by the light
and remembering the coding of my matrix.

Each of my aspects was clear
and my bodies swayed in alignment,
soothing their calling.
They communicated, one to the other,
sharing the perceptions of themselves
and jointly bringing their differences into oneness.
And I rejoiced that it was so.

As I moved, the oneness spoke from me
loudly and softly at once.

My fullness was as a trumpet and a bell,
sounding the resonance of truth.

The people were aware of me, always aware of me,
for the capacity to bear light was great
and they were drawn forward,
they knew not why.

They would follow me as though when I walked
I was giving this light to them,
as, of course, I was.

They would bring me gifts in secret,
not wanting others to know.
They would leave them inside my door frame
without their name upon them,
so that they appeared to come from nowhere,
which was just as well,
for I would not have known
how to receive the gifts
otherwise.

They knew this shyness within me,
the reluctance to join with them in any other way than
through their bodies and their souls.
And they honored this
and did not accost me for discussion or translation,
and they followed me.

Some would hide in the doorways as I passed
and pretend to be abstracted in thought or occupation.

114

Others would be bold until I would turn toward them,
and then they would look away,
after first paying homage to me with their eyes.

These were the ones who were aware of me
and obeyed the voices within
and did not allot me a place in their life
according to the law of the land,
but rather, according to the law of the soul.

They were well rewarded,
for they would receive from my eyes and my presence
the affirmation of light,
the ritual of passage from one soul cell to another
which transcended the limitation of mind and body.

The affirmation of light would release them
from the bonds of the human and allow them,
if for one second,
the experience of again
knowing the light within.
They received the gift
and were well contented.

They would know their calling
and surrender to it,
feeling the return of hope within their chests,
and they would honor me quietly,
for they had no words to speak of it.

And perhaps, in the end, it was the best way.
For it ran true and deep and real,
and there was no way for them to betray it.

THE RABBI'S HEART

I awakened before dawn on the Sabbath. There was no sound, the birds sleeping, the creatures silent. A soft breeze blew upon me from the open window, and I stretched, relaxing into my warm bed cloths.

And then there arose a vision of my father, the rabbi. He was sitting alone in the temple of his people. The temple of his God. He sought the solace of his tradition and faith, the peace that the words of his God imbued.

His lips moved in a silent cadence of sound, sending the rhythm of peace to quiet his grieving heart. But there was no peace—only sadness, only a longing to understand.

If he had been a normal man, if his life's work was not as rabbi, he could leave it be, know that it was out of his hands, pretend there was nothing he could do. But no, he was the spokesperson for the temple, the keeper of the truth of his people.

He did not know what to believe. What was the truth? There was nowhere to go, no one with whom he could speak. His wife? Yes, perhaps, but she, as a woman did not—could not understand his dilemma. He could barely speak of his fears at all, not even to himself.

Who was this Mary? This daughter of his loins? This one who knew God in a way he did not? She challenged his every belief, the very concept of his order. She had knowledge, faith, commitment to God. And yet her God was not his God.

The trees were her God, and the rocks and the water and the stars. She spoke of the Goddess, of the fiber of being, of creation, and of the feminine as divine, and this was not what he lived or believed.

He longed to teach her as a son, to mold her mind to the tradition, to speak to her of the sacred words of the temple. But his tradition forbade it. There was no place for her there.

And she was bold—stridently affirming her truths.
Her truth was stronger than her need for his approval.
She was free—and he envied her.

He sighed, turning the questions over again and again in his heart. For this was where he felt her, and this was where he felt God.
Why would they not come together there? Why could he not find peace in his heart with her and with his God?

He rose to ready himself for temple, directing his mind from habit to do what he must do. But a thought made him pause and consider as he made his way to the altar, a thought that made him stop:

If only she had been a boy. He wished that she had been a boy!

His anguish was real, and his grief and his pain.
He turned toward the altar, and as the rays of dawn touched the silver of the chalice, he saw a rainbow of light.

120

He moved his arm toward the chalice, and as the rainbow touched his outstretched hand, something stirred within him. A presence, a familiar presence lay there in the rainbow upon the chalice. And then he felt the grief in his heart lessen, and leave, and he saw that the rainbow was a bridge which joined him and his daughter and his God in his heart. He felt tears falling upon his hand, and for that instant he and his God and his Mary were one.

If only she had been a boy.

Reunion With Jesus

The Mother Mary came to me one evening,
saying that Jesus had returned from his
years of sojourn in the mountains.
He had asked her about me and
she told him how I had lived
the fulfillment of my calling to heal
for all of the ten years
he had been gone.
She told him of my aloneness,
my fears and my determination
to live the memory of my design.

We had talked then of him.
She told me that he was disturbed,
for he longed to live his calling more fully.
There were so many to help and to heal,
and we were all driven by the same purpose.
Until now, he and I had chosen
to live our callings alone,
and as he asked her for my direction,
he told her it was now time
for us to be together.

She knew that the separation from him
had been difficult for me.

She accorded me her tribute by
coming to give her support and
to prepare me for my reunion with him.
She knew of my path of aloneness,
for she had walked it also,
and so she sat with me
and we supped,
spinning the web of our union
more tightly.

The next night,
when the land lay in stillness,
he came to my home in the garden of Gethsemane.
He knew that the men came here
for healing in the day and the women at night,
and he came to claim me.

He lived cycles of aloneness, and
I had been waiting for him to come back,
for we had much to do together,
and it was time to begin.
Ultimately, there was no one else
but he and I,
for the union of our
male and female
would forge our becoming.

When he arrived, I told my woman, Naomi,
that I was not to be disturbed. She received this message
and asked me no questions, for she knew who he was.
I closed the door then, and faced him.

"And so you have come," I said.

"As you see," he answered.

I was unsure, shy and vulnerable, hesitant to open myself unto him.
For a moment the months and years
stood between us as a wall,
from which we would not venture to join.
And the human was, for a moment, the most prominent part.

But as we stood face to face, we relaxed,
and our hands came out to the other spontaneously.
We placed our palms together,
and we were able to feel the other again.

I felt the weariness of his body, the tiredness,
the aching in his loins,
the deepening faith in his heart.
There was a new reaching in his awareness.
He had grown much.

Our hands became one,
as did our vision, and

we moved one into the other's eyes, and began to travel

forward and backward in time

as   an   arc.

127

Our identities shifted and we saw the plan again.
We played it back and forth in the manner of a
conversation as, of course, it was.

I showed him the resolution of his design:
the crucifixion, the resurrection,
the unfolding of his light
and his purpose to bring unity.
I spoke of his patterns of learning
and his need to trust in me
and in his choices—
the choices he had made in the Swing.

No betrayal—
No need to choose aloneness—
No need now to live apart from me.

We began to see what was next in the design, and
I began to see what I had to do
to help him live his choices.

I drew him forward into the records to show him the plan,
sustaining the energy of his emotional body in harmony
so he would not be affected humanly by what he saw.

I was protecting him, and I knew that I could not give him
this gift of protection later. So I chose to do it now.

We looked ahead to my stoning, which was my crucifixion.
For weeks now the visions had been coming: at night,
during the day, all the time, I was seeing it
over and over again.

Suddenly, the angels spoke to him directly.
I stood and did not listen as they surrounded and encompassed
me in love. I released my will, open to their ministrations.

As I surrendered,
I felt him take my essence in his arms and   lift   it   up,
and then he did the same with my body.

He carried me to my bed
and laid me down,
taking from me the cloths of my body.
The angels instructed him,
and I prepared to receive from him and from them.

He rubbed   my   body   with   oil,
infusing   love   into   the   cells,
giving to me the light I gave to others,
refreshing me,
renewing me.

He spoke to each cell through his mind
and his awareness and his hands.
He spoke of the truth to my cells,
encouraging their wholeness,
releasing their strife,
removing the judgement from them,
supporting them,
pledging loyalty,
stating that he would be there to relieve the pain
and share the joy.

I received it as a balm to the soul and spirit.
I rejoiced in his existence and in our union,
and in the gift I had given myself of
his presence in my life.

We became father/mother, angel/god,
brother/sister, friend/helper,
gentle, tender, giving, and loving.

And in the end, I slept,
and dreamed that we were home,
laughing together with the ones with no names,

and   that   we   were   l i g h t,

and   that   the

                    h u m a n   p a r t

                                        w a s   o v e r.

130

THE FORGING OF
MALE AND FEMALE

Jesus and I held hands and walked into the night.
Since his return from the mountains, we met each day to exchange the
fiber of being and to practice the magic we were here to bring. Tonight
we called the moon to guide our journey, and the stars burned brightly,
affording us companionship.

We walked lightly, drawn by the night and the forces, free of the people.

We felt a weight, sometimes, when we were with them, so much need and
so much pain. When his fear was stronger than his memory, Jesus was
affected by what he saw, and his vibration was dense.

There was so little time. He was reluctant to emerge, and I challenged him.
My soul forced me onward, making me bold, showing me the need for
him to go deeper and trust more and more from the knowledge within
himself so that we could fulfill the design.

It was my calling to forge a union with him, to guide his force of life, and
to assist him in the joining of his consciousness with his body.
I had practiced this forging with Elisabeth at the Sea of Galilee.

I awakened his maleness as the initiation into the sisterhood had
awakened my womanness. Each night as we held hands, he felt energy
rising in his body through his spine.

Joining his consciousness with it, he felt his maleness and his wisdom more completely. His knowledge would come forth, and my womanness would forge it with creation.

And so he learned to create in the world through the balancing of his male and female, the balancing of knowledge and creation. The elements of air, fire, earth and water were in complete union and balance within him. He was a raw gem of wisdom, undefined and unshaped, in a male body. He had not yet refined his knowing for this time or place or these people, and so we merged the knowledge through his cells to ground it into this time and place.

Sometimes he was impatient with the process of learning, thinking of all he had yet to do. He knew the design, and yet, at times, did not seem to know. There were many moments of lucidity, followed by moments when he would withdraw and push me out of his consciousness. Becoming preoccupied, he would retreat into the hills, and I could not reach him.

When he remembered that he had everything he needed within him, he would return to me and reach out and invite me again within. Each time we met he felt more committed and more present, and we experienced the other more completely. Preparing for our work, we learned to trust the other fully, as we taught each other of our calling.

His hands caressed me, now, as we walked, and he spoke to me from his being, sending me rays of light. And I sent the rays back to him, anchoring them in his awareness, as we began to vision our next steps.

My Earthly Sister, Martha

Martha was my younger sister, and I loved her. I was five years older than she, and often my mother let me care for her. We had grown together, playing and laughing and exploring the world as children.

As she grew, I taught her of the world and showed her the pathways of being. Our rooms were one beside the other, and we would talk through the wall, joking and sharing, long after our parents had gone to bed.

When she was in the time of her blooming, and I was beginning my healing work, she watched the men and women coming to me for the recognition of their souls, and she began to be jealous of me, even as I showed her the ways of my calling.

She compared herself to me, not understanding that we were both a necessary part of the design, each having an equally important role to play in the outcome. She did not love or trust herself, and so she did not love or trust me.

Sometimes when she was in her room, she would look at herself in the mirror, and as I passed by, I would see her watching me out of the corner of her eye. At night when she had long since been put to bed, I would feel her eyes upon me, watching me. I was not sure if she was present with me through her dreams, or if she had a portal through which she stared at me in the dark of the night.

When Jesus came, she would go to him and tarry there. She followed him, sometimes for many hours. Loving her as a sister, he would play with her when he was not abstracted in thinking, and she would honor the time that he spent with her, cherishing him greatly.

Then as she grew, she envied the time he and I spent together and questioned me about it. Although she was with us, she did not know the great design, and I could not tell her. There was too much at stake, and it was not my place.

She sensed my withholding and became more and more distrustful. I watched her change from a sensitive, innocent, insecure young woman to a mistrustful one—more and more insensitive, more and more demanding.

She became vain and haughty and challenging. I knew it was a defense, and yet she would not let me share my love with her, and she grew more and more bitter.

She begrudged me my power, my knowledge, and my calling, and did not follow her own design.

A constant source of irritation for me, chafing against the grain of my being, she challenged my love of the ones I most treasured.

I knew I must keep my own counsel, must give her only the love of one sister to another, even though I knew the design—perhaps, in the end, because I knew the design. It meant that I must love her regardless of her action, or I would go against my own calling.

The angels had shown me what would happen if I held up a shield of protection against her. I knew I must not protect myself, regardless of her actions. And yet I knew that there would be moments when not to do so would make me vulnerable, would make me appear as a coward or a fool.

Humility, the humbleness of my learning.

Even as I mistrusted her, I admired her. She was tempestuous, beautiful, and passionate. She did not have to answer for any other soul, only her own. Thus she was less cautious than I, taking what she wanted without feeling disgrace in what she created. She acted without conscience and felt excused from responsibility.

She was a temptress, seductive and brazen, taking the qualities of the sensuous and making them sexual. And yet she could appear gentle and soft and replete with knowing. She lived the dichotomy of humanness fully.

She wanted what I had, not because she really wanted it, but because I had it. Without a true sense of loving with those I cared for, she wanted only to match my strength, my power, and my abilities.

She did not understand why I was with the people and interpreted the closeness I had with them as an action against her.

She was my sister, and yet in the true sense of the word, she was not. For she did not respect me, or yearn for companionship with me, or share, or create with me. She did not support me and nurture me and care for me as a true one of womanness.

She was my sister, and yet the blood we shared was a source of pain and competition and created in me a longing for separation. I wanted to cut my heart away from hers so that different blood would run in her veins, and I would be free of her taunting.

Once, I let go of my rage at her, and she let go of hers at me. I asked her what she wanted, and she said, "I want your soul. I want your life. I want to do what you do and be what you are and have them love me the way they love you! Why can I not have this also?"

And then I knew there was nothing I could do. She struggled and competed with me, not listening to her soul's message, not honoring her own calling, forgetting that we are all one soul.

Although I loved her, all I could do was live my life and let her be. I knew not how long it would take, or how it would be lived, but I knew that one day we would come to love and acknowledge the other—knew the design would bring us union. And so I blessed her and myself, and I let it all go, for there was nothing else I could do.

THE HUMAN AND THE DIVINE

Jesus always came to me at sunset when the veil was thin and the devas were singing at the completion of their day. This night we joined hands and walked into the hills and sat quietly in the shadows of the rabbi's garden.

Each day he gave me permission to enter his awareness and to lead him into the space of the void. We practiced bringing the dimensions together to dispel the illusion of life and death.

We knew that if Jesus feared death, then he did not trust the design, and trusting the greater plan and his part in it was essential to his mission.

So I taught him to remember the immortality of his soul and to experience his soul within his body. I told him of the plan and reminded him of the design.

At times he resisted me, and his fear rested between us, visible in his eyes. He was no longer surprised that I knew immediately when his fear returned again and when he withdrew his permission to continue.

This night, he dropped his hands in frustration.
I sat quietly, not speaking, breathing patiently into myself.

"Why am I so afraid?" he asked.
"What is it that stops me from the knowing? Why do I not trust?
I can go so far, and then—well, you know. You always know.
And that, sometimes, makes it more difficult."

"Yes." I said. "You almost wish I could not see it."

It was a statement, not a question. I knew he was angry with me at times
because I remembered the design. And he was so preoccupied with what
he thought he did not know, that he was unable to see my struggles, and
my questions, and my aloneness.

Often, when we practiced moving into the void it would take all night, and
so I did not hurry. I knew him as I knew myself, and I was patient. He still
did not trust me fully, for he did not trust himself. His mind convinced
him of the danger in trusting the unseen, and so I continued to make the
unseen more visible to him, more palpable.

The time was approaching when he would change his perception,
had to do so, to stay within the design. He knew this,
for he was concentrating now, with intention and choice.

He was determined, and he took my hands again.
I closed my eyes and began to deepen my breathing. As he watched,
he breathed also, matching each of his breaths with mine.
I began drawing him into the void, deep within the center of his body.

As I drew him with my breath, he opened slowly,
and I urged him to let go more and more.
His mind strongly controlled his reality,
and he knew he could not vision until he let go, and
he was caught in the pain of that dichotomy.

I sent him encouragement through my breath and lifted him into
creation, lessening the control of his mind and helping him to reach
into the truth.

I felt him move deeper
into the darkness of the void,
his breath quickening suddenly.
He steeled himself
as if against the onslaught of an invisible enemy.
His awareness cried out to me silently,
and his heart pulled me into him.
I went willingly,
knowing there was nothing to fear,
knowing there is never really anything to fear.

He held fast to me
and I stayed with him,
continuing to lift him silently
from the void into the light.

He hesitated,

R I G H T   O N   T H E   B R I N K.

I directed my power,
matching his awareness to mine
to carry him forward.

A N D   H E   D I E D,

his breath going out of his body.

And he

hung

between   worlds.

The pain of his race
and of all the races
rose as a wave of force throwing him back,
and he tottered for a moment
on the brink of eternity.

I sent him the vision and the essence of the design,

and he caught it.

He saw the plan,
the hologram
of the coming together
of all ages and all races
into unity.

It was the truth of why he had come
and what he would do.
And the knowing
of all time
cried out to him
to merge with the design.

He saw his choices clearly,
knew his true identity,
and remembered he was all souls
living in all time.

And finally,
    finally,
        he **knew** that **there**isno**se**paration.

And when he merged with that knowing,

h e   w a s   b o r n   a g a i n.

He drew a breath
which wracked his body
and tore asunder the fear
and the pain of duality
and brought him

H o m e   A g a i n   I n t o   B e i n g

into   the   knowledge   that   there   is   no   death.

And the light of his intention
joined with the light of his
c a l l i n g.

We floated in the dimensions
called transition
for a time.

We saw the light and the dark,
the people and the beings.
We saw the peoples' choices
reflected in the halls of time,
and we acknowledged their struggle for truth.
We saw how close the answers were to them,
and that the answers were in a place
they did not think to look, within themselves.

And we pledged, together, to bear unto them the light.

It was a deepening of our commitment to them,
and therefore to ourselves
and each other.

We breathed the truth of the order of being
and shone it as a light upon the people,
drawing them into their divinity.

We saw all time and all space
and drew upon the force of life,
anchoring it into our experience
so the magic would accompany us.

We infused the light of spirit
into the density of form
and merged them
to ease our mission.

And the light spread, and caught, and held.

And the future showed us that
our vibration affected the people.
Hope touched their hearts and their memories,
and they awakened
renewed and refreshed
on their journeys.

We joined hearts
and flew through the universe,
reaffirming our connection to God,
to mankind,
and to each other.

A new sparkle was in our awareness,
heightening our experience,
drawing all magical forces
into being with us.

Then we listened to the council
of the Hierarchy of Order.
They instructed us and
drew us into infinite space,
forging more and more light into each of us,
reassuring us and supporting us,
explaining with infinite patience
the divine order of the moments to be.

We relaxed within their divine arms
and knew our purpose and our path
and the best way to accomplish it.

And before we left them, they gave us each a gift.

My gift was a headdress of crystal starlight,
woven into the strands of my hair,
overlying my third eye
in the center of my forehead,
giving me continued vision,
bathed in rainbows of light.

They called it **Hope**
as they placed it gently on my head.

The gift they gave to Jesus
was a matrix of pure gold,
a scepter
which they placed within his heart,
the symbol of the Christ.
They called it **Love**.
A cosmic beacon,
it drew to him the life of all the kingdoms
through the fiber of being.
He had completed his lessons,
for the kingdoms now pledged to him
their assistance.

It was a moment of recognition
and of merging the bases of power.
Now we were as one power:
male and female.

Our forging of this truth
between male and female
brought the balance of power into union.

Soon I would outwardly yield my power to his
and I knew it was time for this yielding,
for my celestial mothers, the stars, gave me vision to see it.

They showed me the matriarchy
and the power of the feminine path
yielding outwardly to the masculine path.

And they spoke to us, saying:

In the beginning of Earth time, the people lived the feminine path, learning of the Earth and her nurturance, the invisible substance of creation. Then the path changed and the people lived the masculine, the power of the word, the choice to think, the choice to give power only to the visible.

The people named the invisible substance, calling it God, making it visible through law and religion, placing it away from themselves, seeking to find the power outside of them, creating in matter.

They strived to mold others, fighting to gain control through the word and the sword, for the power of the world is lived through the molding of others to conform to the same truth.

The people will first feel separation, to later recognize the union of the dichotomies. The union of these opposites will come only after the people know war and choose peace; only after they know power and choose truth. . . .

For their choices will bring to them the knowing of their inner wisdom and the memory of their oneness.

As Christ and I listened, we knew that we lived our power through the choice to remember the way of truth—the acknowledgment that all truth, ultimately, is the same, and leads us into oneness.

For the only truth is union. . . .

We awoke in each other's arms,
not knowing when we had moved or slept.
We stared into each other's eyes;
now no barriers,
no mistrust,
no questions.

Tears welled in our eyes
and flowed over our faces
and down our bodies,
merging the trust
the knowing
and the being.

His hand tenderly stroked my face, and he said,
"Thank you for loving me as you do
and taking me to the places that you go.
I am what I am because you are."

"And I am because you are," I said.

We nestled into the hillside
as the mists of the night descended,
covering us with cloaks of dew.

The guardians of the night stood around us,
and the stars continued to bless us
as we prepared to sleep again.

The devas softened the ground where we lay,
making the rocks into pillows of velvet moss
beneath us.

And when we awoke again, we knew that
when our prophecy was complete
the world would be different:
the flowers blooming
and the ground healed.

In earnest now, would we spread the magic.
We would touch the hearts of the people
and open their consciousness.
This place called Earth
would truly be their home,
and they would belong to their world,
to their souls,
and to each other.

We slept deeply and restfully,
dreaming of flowers dancing in starlight,
kissed by the rays of multi-colored planets.
And we knew it would be many moons
before we slept like this again.

I RECEIVE FROM CHRIST

His visit was unexpected
and his timing was perfect.
It was midday and I was alone.

He strode in full of energy, free-moving,
breathing fully. I looked at him closely.
I had never seen him like this.

Christ said, "I have come just to visit with you. Always, when we are
together you are working and straining to teach me and take me
I know not where! Not today. Today I want to share joy with you!"

He began to grin at me and laughed suddenly, saying,
"You are always so serious."

He came toward me, and I stood very still.
For the first time he was taking control,
and I felt a rush of tenderness and fear and longing.
I wanted him more in that moment than ever before,
and yet I knew I must transcend my desire.

He came yet closer.
Reaching out his hand, he gently pulled the hair back from
the nape of my neck, close to my head.

His hand brushed my skin,
and I shivered involuntarily.

He stopped his smiling.

We stood very close,
and yet our bodies did not touch.
I let out my breath, unaware that I had held it.

He said, "Do you fear me, then?"

I felt his concern, and then I felt his awareness
grasp and hold the answer.

It was his turn to sigh. He dropped his arm to his side.
"What are we to do, my Mary?" he asked.

"We are to do nothing," I said, "for it is not necessary to do anything
with our love. It is enough only to live it."

"What do the records show about this?" he asked.

I paused, taking my time, remembering and reflecting.

"I have been shown that we merge as fields of energy, as lights. I have
seen us sharing love as no two other mortals can share love in this time,
transcending the human, loving unconditionally.

"I have seen you holding me, touching me, and loving me, and I have seen that you will not enter me or plant your seed in my womb or any womb, not as the one Christ. Your essence is the embodiment of the perfect balance of the male and female, and your calling is to live that balance completely unto yourself. Living it will show the people that the unity their souls desire is within them."

He searched my face and knew I spoke the truth, and he sighed again. "Yes," he said, "that is what I have seen also."

He looked away from me, staring for a moment out the window at the brightness of the noonday sun. I felt him sifting the feelings, the desires, and the knowing, and then he looked back at me and said,
"And so we can feel joy?"

He smiled, and I relaxed. He brought my head to rest upon his chest, and we stood thus, for a time, together.

And then he said, "Tell me of your soul's journey, my Mary.
I have taken so much and given so little."
He was serious, and I felt his full attention upon me, waiting.

He was so purposeful, so present for me. Now he seemed ready to join his life with mine and to share the design with me, not through worry or fear, but through love and friendship and caring.

All at once the weight of the years of aloneness overwhelmed me,
the years when he had stayed away and kept me from him.

I sobbed, and he held me without questions.
I let the weight run through my body,
and I was touched with pain.

I cried out with each memory,
and he stayed with me
as I had done with him.
He felt my pain and transformed it with light.
He merged with me as I moved through each memory,
so that I would know that I was not alone.

I gave thanks to the lights and the Gods
and the angels that he was there with me.

My tears flowed, cleansing the wounds within.
Then I felt him send light deep inside me
to replace the dark memories of fear and separation.
As I released the memories,
the light filled me
and my cells began to dance
as joy flooded my being.
I rejoiced in the wisdom of the design
and gave thanks for this moment.

When I felt calmer, he began to tease me,
wiping my tears away with his beard
very deliberately,
as I had sometimes wiped his feet with my hair.

He made faces to amuse me
and to make me laugh.

He swung me in circles, holding my waist, humming to me,
inviting me to dance and move and rejoice.
And so we danced, the pain gone, the joy flowing between.

And when I was tired from the dancing and could not catch my breath,
he lay me down on the cloths, and we laughed and laughed,
holding our sides and shaking our heads.

Later, as we grew quiet, he sang to me the lullabies of the people, stroking
my brow and my face and my hair. His voice brought to me a feeling of
safety, and after a time I drifted into sleeping. I remembered the same
feeling when my mother had held me to her breast as a child, weaving the
beating of her love into the beating of my heart.

For the first time, Christ had felt my pain and heard my grief.
In the way of the human he had seen my tears and dried them, taken my
burdens and lifted them. He had been with me as had my mother, in
tenderness and softness, judging me not, allowing for me my humanness,
loving me still.

And in that moment I loved him more than ever before.

THE TRANSFERENCE OF POWER

I felt the judgement of the people upon me,
h e a v y, as a w e i g h t,
their lack of understanding surpassed only by their hatred.

The judgement was as
d a g g e r s within my soul,
coming again and again
in waves.

There was no way out, I must go through it. I knew that.
I could not run, could not hide, but must go forward with the plan and
allow the resolution to be effected.

I breathed into my body
and felt the soul seed within my chest
and drew upon it
into the place of my being,
my true identity.

I drew deeply
and more deeply inward
to the seed of light,
gathering,
g a t h e r i n g strength,

forging the connection
with the wisdom from within,
knowing there was no other place to find it.

They were coming for me,
gathering their force,
preparing to slay me,
and it would be
almost too late by the time he found me.
I knew he loved me, but that he would hesitate
because it would be the declaration of his place here,

       his coming out.

It would make him v i s i b l e.

It would all begin in earnest.
It would all begin.

The rocks would signal the need for truth,
bringing him, finally,
into the light of his calling.

It had been so designed, but I was afraid nonetheless.

The pain I reckoned upon was not the physical hurt,
but the psychic damage they
would inflict on me.
Invading my soul with their anger
they would call me e v i l—
piercing my defenses.

THIS WAS MY CRUCIFIXION.

By design, my crucifixion was to be the

moment of his recognition:

the heroic moment of his coming out,
declaring his power,
calling upon his force.

It was our transference of power,
a giving-over of the torch.

For now, they would follow him instead of me,
call to him in the night from their souls instead of me.
The base of power would shift from female to male
and remain so for 2000 years.

My life would never be the same.
I would follow him in public,
and counsel him in private,
playing the role of repentant sinner.
Attending only as he directed,
I would follow, now humble,
appearing to attend his every word,
following the design,
surrendering to the greater will and the higher good,
knowing he could not do it without me.

Seeing my lesson over and over again
in each face, in each set of eyes,
every time they looked at me, I would learn
of humbleness again and again.

169

I poured sacred essences and oils upon my body,
massaging my flesh deeply. I spoke to my body and
prepared it for the onslaught.
And I prayed.

I burned the cedar and the sage of purity and asked to be guided.

I called to the Goddess and the Gods and the masters of all time
and the ones with no names and prayed for the courage to live the design.

I opened my arms   w i d e   to the sky
and invited the moon
to rest within my breast

to l i g h t m y w a y.

I anchored the golden ray within my consciousness,
the ray of the Mother and the Father.
And then I rested,

                    and waited.

MY STONING

I told Naomi to leave that night but she would not, sleeping by my side and caring for me as a child. The Mother Mary and my earthly mother visited me in the night also bringing comfort and strength, for they knew what was to come. They sat with me for a time, leaving while darkness still lay present, but my woman would not leave me.

The men began to gather outside my door at dawn, a few at first, and then more and more, looking for a fight, a way to vent their anger. Naomi and I heard their loud voices, their numbers building as their hatred grew.

When I knew I could hold it off no longer, I went to meet them. "What do you want here?" I shouted to them. "Why have you come here to my home?" They were taken aback. They were gathering their force to break down my door and pillage my home, and that I would not allow.

They answered me roughly, according me no rights, judging me and sentencing me without trial, calling me a seductress—a sorceress. A daughter who is not sanctioned by her earthly father is judged rightfully by the people, so they thought.

I was surprised that they feared me, but I knew it was so when I showed myself to them first, taking control. They had come to stone me out of their fear of my actions with the people. They would not have been disturbed if my healing had not been powerful and meaningful. I would have been no threat to them.

They shouted names at me, their faces dark with hatred and anger. I was stoic and this fueled their anger further. The froth of their hatred boiled over.

This hatred needed reciprocating or there was nothing to fuel it. Three of the men lunged forward and grabbed me, their fingers making marks of red upon my arms. They dug in their nails to have me cry out or curse them. But I did nothing. I would not hate them.

One of the men hit me in the face, drawing blood across my mouth. He pulled my hair and mocked me. I had prepared myself, and yet I was struck deep within as if I were branded, and perhaps I was. I prayed as I always did when I became afraid—when the world is clearer than the spirit—for I knew if I allowed these men to become my reality, I would lose myself in their illusion and fear and forget the truth of why I was here and what I had come to do.

As I began praying, they held me more tightly, sensing that I was less afraid. They thought they could hold me there and make me the victim of their will, but I knew there are no victims, and I chose to meet my destiny with steadfastness and courage.

The crows came around me then, the birds of my calling, the ones who bring unseen knowledge. They cawed loudly, alighting in the trees of my garden.

At first these men wished to harm me because I did not comply with their laws and their ways. They needed power to fight the demons within themselves, and they felt powerless.

They no longer lived according to the truth within them. They hated me because I was the mistress of my soul, and they had not found their souls.

The crows, the keepers of the sacred law, cawed loudly again reminding me of what the Mother Mary had said to me at the time of my initiation so many years ago: "Know that the truth is encoded within the people and that they will find it. See them always, Mary, as if they are remembering it, and know that what you do helps them such to do."

And so I looked at them—chose to see them. I had not done so before. I had reacted to them as a mob, not allowing myself to be there completely. I had not seen them as individuals. Perhaps, if I did?

I began to look at them, one by one, and found I did not know most of them. The ones who came to me for healing were not here. There was no one of my village here whom I had known in a personal way.

I acknowledged this gratefully as I looked at these men, and I felt compassion. They did not know their calling, did not know who they were or why they had come. They felt no blessing in this world for them. They had forgotten their divinity.

The crows cawed again, telling me that beliefs that limit mankind are illusion, and I acknowledged another passage of my learning.

Then the men released my arms suddenly, forming a circle around me, neither touching me nor letting me go.

They were undecided. I had done nothing to them. There were rumors about me breaking the laws of tradition, healing by touch and sound, but they had no evidence against me. They wanted me to bow to their tradition, but I could not. I could not bow to anyone or anything except the Gods. And they did not know the Gods and the Goddesses, they knew only the one male deity which made me unequal to them and gave them the right to make me obey.

I was in the most powerful position, the center of the circle. They realized this as the energy began to build. They knew they could not back down now and yet they did not know what to do. There was less hatred, but they did not know why. Their determination to hurt me was less keen, but they did not know why. I sensed them acknowledge that hurting me would not help them, would not make their lives happier—that killing me would not make them happy.

They were restless. Some continued to taunt me, but most were silent, shifting uncomfortably from one foot to the other, looking at each other with a growing uneasiness.

Then one of the men decided to finish what they had started. He picked up a rock, screaming names at me. Some of the others joined him, picking up rocks, raising their voices, taunting me.

The first man raised his arm and shouted that I must pay for my sins. I had seen his face in my vision, and so I was prepared.

He raised his arm and threw his rock, but it landed wide of the mark, for another man hit his arm, throwing off his aim. A fight started as this happened, the men's anger sparked now, the two men pushing each other. This convinced them that I was evil—their turning against one another had to be my doing. And so their focus shifted again to me. The ones with rocks took aim. Others began picking them up.

Three men grabbed me again, pushing and pulling me this way and that, fighting the other through my body because I would not fight or run or protest. They shouted, their anger bursting the air, fueled by the knowledge that they were acting with no conscience.

Suddenly, as the men were about to throw me to the ground and pelt me with rocks, a voice cut across the noise shouting boldly,

"He among you who has not judged, cast the first stone!"

A hush fell across the mob.

Looking up I saw Christ and his disciples standing at the edge of the circle. He sent Thomas and Peter quickly to my side, and the men who held me melted into the circle, unprotesting.

I was disheveled and bruised and sore, but unscathed. Christ knew this at a glance and addressed the men who were poised to strike. Some of them aimed their rocks at him and the disciples at his side. He displayed no fear and no judgement. They knew instinctively that he would make it possible for them to act differently without losing their pride.

"This one here," he said, indicating me with his arm, "has come to this Earth to learn about judgement, and so you are teaching her." There was laughter here and there in the crowd.

"Who among you wishes to be judged? Whoever you are, step now into the circle. If you have never judged, never thought of judging, step now into the circle."

He waited, looking at each man one by one.
"I know you, all of you. You are not here to judge and condemn the people of your body. You are here to live and work and have your children and find your souls and create happiness in this place of the Earth. And you are learning, for that is why you have come here. You are learning through the ways of humanity, as is she.

"She is bold, is she not?" He waited, and the crowd shouted, "Yes, yes!"
"What is the sentence to be for boldness, I ask you?"
There was no answer from the crowd.

"She is beautiful, is she not? What is the sentence to be for beauty?"
Again there was no response from the crowd, and he continued,
"She is willful as a wild horse! What is the sentence to be for willfulness?"

One by one he broke through the prejudice and the opinion and the judgement, making each statement more absurd than the last.

"She is different! What is to be the sentence for this?" He waited.

"If there is no one here who can determine her sentence, I propose to you that she go free. For as with you, life will teach her what it is that she has come to learn. Her life will do what you can not do."

He looked at them one by one, and said, "Remember that you are Jews, and that this woman is also a Jew. She brings light to your people and healing to your wives and sisters. Her ways are different from the ways of man, but she threatens not man. Her ways are bold and willful, but of pure intent. If there is none among you who can rightfully sentence her or withstand the judgement of your people, then go now to your homes and make today a celebration that you acted with knowing, according this one the right to live her life in the way of her calling. Do not take from her what it is not your right to take. No one has the right to make another live their truth. Are we not in rebellion now about this for our people? When we judge, we are then judged."

He moved quickly to my side, and taking my arm, walked with me to my door. The disciples made a wall around us, and the crowd began to disperse. We were silent for a time, all in thought, our bodies trembling for what had almost come to pass. And then, as the men moved down the road, they talked again about normal things, asking each other about health and work and family.

And the tension broke, for they could take from themselves the stigma of stoner, murderer, aggressor, perpetrator, and become again who they were, who they knew themselves to be, and they were grateful.

Naomi and my sisters who had gathered met us at the door. They took me inside and held me, each one, and then laid me down and washed my face and body, combed my hair, changed my robe, and made me comfortable.

And before I slept I felt Christ's eyes upon me from the door frame, and I looked up.
"My Mary, rest in peace."

"I almost did," I said, and we smiled, letting it all go. In his eyes was the tribute and in mine the gratitude, and as the women watched, we sent this honoring back and forth. And then he inclined his head to me and was gone.

I Danced On The Mountain

I danced on the mountain
and I was alone,

and then they would come to me,

and then I would be alone,

and then they would come to me.

And they descended from heaven

the angels,

and we intertwined our wings,

gently touching,

and the times of glory

would rest within the moment

of the Earth's time,

and all would come together.

And we began to

s   y

w   a

to the rhythm
of the Earth
as she turned

on   axis
her

and all the kingdoms danced with us
in accord.

We went
        forward
                with the current
                        of the wave
                                of all the water
                                        upon the
                                                Earth.

The
mountains
gave access
to their power
and we merged with it,
drawing the flame from
the center of the Earth.

The flow of night
　　　　　felt hot
　　　as if lava
　　　　flowed over us
　　　　　　　and encouraged our dance.

Andtherewas**noseparation**from**allthespheres.**

As
   we danced
         more and more
                     light
                 d
                   e
                     s
                       c
                         e
                           n
                             d
                               e
                                 d

                         to join us,

      and we celebrated the night.

            More and more of the lights
                were bringing
                 to the Earth
               the calling of order
               and issuing song,

                   inaudible

            to the people's ears,
         heard only by their hearts.

As
they
dreamed,
they saw
the angels
and heard the song
and felt the oneness,
and began to remember why they had come.
They would awaken in the morning, softer
and more dear.
And the substance of the Earth was enriched
and began to reflect the dance
as it joyfully filled its essence
with the song and the light
and the current
of the force
of the life
which
abounded
within
it.

And we joined with the fragrance of the flowers
and the light of the stars
and the spaces of being
from which all things
are born.

187

There was a dance, meaning
an accord of all energies and aspects
into oneness.

And we merged and blended our essences
so that I,
human and spirit,
became

l i g h t .

It was a gift of the heavens
and the dance was an affirmation of my belonging
and the wings of the angels brushed my wings
and we felt the pleasure of the touching.

The sensation was as the first drop of rain
on a hot, parched day,
the first kiss of life from a sunrise.

As I danced
I felt the joy
of flying without feet
to hold me down

the gift of joy
and freedom
of light-filled bliss
of remembering
the design

and the wings upheld me

as I lay down to rest.

And I was soothed
as if by feathers
brushing lightly
over the skin
of my body.

And as I went to sleep,
the song was sung in my ear
of the voices
of one thousand beings of light
enfolding me
in the love of eternity.

And I knew God.

THE TRUTH

It was a fine spring day. The wind chased the clouds across the pure blue of the sky, bringing a warm breeze to us as we sat in my garden.

The disciples and Christ and I had just finished the noonday meal and were joking together, the sound of our laughter drifting beyond the garden gate.

I looked up to see a child of our village, carried by her mother and father, and I stopped my laughing. It was known that we gathered here on the Sabbath, and the people would oft times bring to us their sick or their dying, and these people had come such to do.

There was a sudden hush as we saw them and felt their anguish.

Without speaking we made room for them before us on the table. The disciples helped Naomi remove the remains of the meal, and I went quickly into my home and brought forth a cloth and laid it upon the table. The mother and father placed their daughter upon it.

The child's mother spoke to Christ, saying, "Master, I have listened to the stories of the people and heard of the miracles you perform. I have prayed to God and asked for the healing of my daughter, and I have received no answer. She remains yet sick. I come to you, for I know that there is nothing more I can do. There is nothing more that anyone can do."

She stopped, overcome with the grief of one who faces absolute loss, and then resumed speaking through the tears in her throat, "You are the only one who can help us."

Christ inclined his head to me, and I placed my hands on the child. I spoke to her soul the message that she was light and that she could choose to remain in the body as light. I spoke to her soul of my love and of the love of the others present. I stayed with my hands on her chest in the place of the soul until I felt her soul respond to me. Then I inclined my head to Christ.

"The soul of your daughter now listens to you, mother. Sit here beside her and speak to her of your love, and we shall begin," Christ said to her gently, guiding her to sit at the side of her daughter.

The woman looked at him in surprise. She had come here to see Christ perform a miracle for her child. She did not know what this had to do with her, did not understand how she could help. But she was afraid, and her hope was gone, and she was not here because she believed, only because she did not. And so she did as he bade her.

We all took up our places, forming a circle around Christ and the mother and the father and the body of the child who lay within. Peter and James and John stood at her head, and Thomas and Simon and Matthew stood at her feet.

The father was restless and unsure and full of fear. I held out my hand to him and he took it. I placed his hand in the center of the chest of his daughter, over her seed of light, and then I reached my hand across the table and took the hand of the mother and laid it on top of the hand of her husband, placing my hand on top of their hands. Judas and Andrew and James were across from me, on either side of the mother and Christ. Philip, Thaddaeus, and Bartholomew stood on either side of me. We placed all of our hands on the body of the child, forming a circle of light.

The child's soul was making a choice, and Christ explained this to the mother and the father as we sent light and the force of life into the cells of her body. Regardless of her choice to stay or to go, the light and life would help her to heal.

Christ said to the parents, "Your child has come here to teach and to learn, as have each of us here gathered. She has come here to fulfill her purpose, and when she has finished what she has come to learn and teach and fulfilled the purpose she has chosen, she will return to her Father and Mother above. You are her parents, but she does not belong to you. She has her own knowing, and you must ask her what she has chosen at this moment."

He inclined his head to the child, saying, "She is now in the pathways beyond the physical body, and you can speak with her only through the love that you hold for her in your hearts. We are sending to her the recognition of light so that she will know that she can live here on Earth and maintain that light. When she was brought forth, she was not taught of the light and her heart and lungs have filled with the fluid of longing for the affirmation of that light."

He looked at the father and said to him, "It is the same pain that you carry in your heart; the pain of living in separation from what you feel and from what you know." The father inclined his head very slightly, unshed tears standing in his eyes.

"When we are separate from our knowing and from those we love and choose to live apart from the love of all peoples, we begin to die, that is to live without life, without joy. There are many reasons why your child may choose to return home, and you must ask her of them."

I said to the parents, "Speak to her from your hearts. She will hear you without words. Tell her of your love and of your learning, and she will attend you."

Christ looked at me then, and we passed the love between us and held it steady, raising the vibration of light within the circle. We spoke one to the other through the light, of time and space and life and the circle of being which never ends. We wove the circle between, carrying the child with us to see the infinite light which she carried within her, showing her the reason for the human living.

And she saw us and acknowledged what we showed her and stopped her journey along the pathway, attending us. The love and the pain of her parents were made known to her, and she accorded them.

Under my hands I felt the quickening, and we all breathed deeply, sending more light and raising her vibration to bring more life into her cells.

She shuddered, her body shook, and she moaned, her sound growing loud and full of pain. The mother became frightened and withdrew, but the father knew, and he spoke aloud, saying, "Yes, let the pain come forth. Let it be gone from within you, my child. Let out the demon of aloneness and pain and fear." And he said to her, "I love you. You have taught me to love."

And then the tears flowed down his face, unheld, and his daughter retched. Peter turned her head as the fluids poured from her mouth; and as her body shook, it released the pain and the fear and the aloneness which it had held, as her father had said. And then her body began to take in the light.

And Christ said to the mother, "Do not be afraid. Come yet closer and speak with your child from your heart, for she has chosen to remain here with you." The mother looked at her daughter again and moved closer to her, disbelief and fear yielding to the hope that perhaps her daughter was choosing to live.

Christ inclined his head to us, and we began to balance her levels—the body, emotion, mind and spirit, bringing them into oneness. After a time her shuddering ceased, and calmness grew, the knowing within her at peace.

I called to Naomi and bade her bring water and cloths, and we bathed the child and changed her and covered her.

She slept there in the garden with the nature spirits and the kingdoms, and we spoke quietly, giving the mother and the father food and drink and love.

Before dark the child awakened, her breathing deep and rhythmed, her color pink, her body full of life. And then we moved her within my home, and her mother and father spoke words of joy with her.

And Christ and I and the disciples went into the garden and held hands in a circle, giving thanks to the lights for their gift to us all: the gift of the circle of life and love which is forever.

THE WATERFALL

One day Christ came to me and said,
"My Mary, I am taking you away to the place of the waters. We must
restore our souls and be alive together in the way of our love's calling, for
it is the last time it will be as such for you and me in this place of Israel."

I knew he spoke the truth, for the design of the resurrection was upon us.
We had been to the waters as children and had spoken often of returning
there again, and so I went, for we did not have much time left together.

We went to the north country, leaving the disciples in Tiberias, making
our way to the place of the waters called Baniass. It was a time of rest from
the healing and the teaching. Because we were examples for the people,
we were watched continually and we needed time to gather our strength
and to prepare for what was to come.

Our journey took several days and we did not hurry, honoring the time
alone. We made our way north, always aware of the land and the force and
the elements. We approached the area of Baniass at noon on the third day
and stopped to eat and rest, taking several more hours to reach our
journey's end.

The cave of the Nature God, Pan, was a distance above the waters of
Baniass. Pan's presence brought knowledge of the kingdoms into the
molecules of water which flowed over the falls and into the streams and
rivers of Israel. When we were young, its beauty had left us breathless.

We had felt the reverence of life there, and the closeness of the kingdoms had filled us with awe. The force of the water and the God, Pan, that powered it, represented to us the marriage of nature and spirit, and we were eager to return.

We heard the water of the falls long before we saw them. We made our way upstream, the sound of the water urging us onward. The water beside us was a deep, rich green—the color of emeralds touched by starlight. As we walked, we saw the molecules of water dancing in the stream, and we heard them laughing and playing. There was a sacredness to the water which was acknowledged by the land, thus making the land sacred also.

We heard the roar of the falls more and more loudly as we approached. At last we were there. It was magnificent! Brilliant in the afternoon sun, two streams merged to create a forceful column of water which dropped many feet into the emerald pool below. The pool narrowed at its base, creating a beautiful stream carrying water throughout the land.

We sat on flat rocks beside the pool with our bare feet in the cool water, holding hands until the last rays of the sun cast golden shadows on the water, touching our shoulders and warming our bodies.
We sat silently, feeling the power and the solace of this place.

Later, when the moon began to shine, we rose, washed the dust of the journey from our bodies, and prepared to sleep.

We stayed beside the pool, in the place of the waters, for three days, leaving only to gather food. Our days were filled with swimming and playing, talking and sharing, loving and holding the other.
We learned from the Gods and Goddesses how to merge with the fields of force and practiced each day in the pool, breathing and merging with the water and the elements.

On the afternoon of our last day, we sat together beside the pool and held hands, joining our hearts in love, affirming our divinity and our oneness with all kingdoms. And as Christ had said, the waters cleansed us and restored our souls.

Then, Christ took the cloths of my body and laid them aside, and I took the cloths of his body and laid them aside, and we took hands and entered the pool, breathing together as we plunged into the water. We swam to the place where the water of the falls met the water of the pool.

We entered the waterfall and the world became
clear water. We were too close to see its color.
We were the water, and yet we continued to breathe,
the air and the water merging within us.

We were one with the water,
the sky, our God, and each other.
There were no boundaries,
no beginning and no end.

The maleness of him reached
within me and filled me,
and my womaness reached into
and filled each male cell,
merging and merging
over and over. . . filling us.

Every moment the tempo rose.
The vibration heightened
and we were carried on the wave,
knowing each other and all things.

I lay on his chest, having two hearts,
his and mine.
They were intertwined,
the male and female,
filling both sides of my chest
and his.

We exchanged stories of the heart,
sharing our journeys
through the current which charged
between us, forging our oneness.

We spoke not with words,
for the droplets of water from the falls
ran within our mouths and throats.
We exchanged air and water
in our lungs
and became fish and fowl
and mammal, and all manner of life
flowed between us.

As we merged, we expanded,
becoming all that is
and no-thing at the same time.

The beat of our hearts
became the beat of the world
and the sky and all Gods,
and we wept.
And our tears
were the gift of our souls
joining with the fluids
of the universe.

The water caressed our bodies,
careening over us,
and our cells embraced it without boundary.

Our bodies became lighter,
and the density flowed away
into the pool
and down the stream.
We were alone with our infiniteness:
immortal, no maleness, no femaleness, no role, no identity,
no separation,
no distinction.

As our bodies flowed away
we were free to unify
as energy
and, as such,
were carried into a state
of pure "being."

It felt like death:
formless,
open,
totally free. . . .
And in that instant
I knew
creation.

Our mouths were joined,
and the breath
and the water
and the immensity
of our being
and our feeling
moved back and forth
between us.

Our merging was ethereal,
and so it remained.
There was no need of anything else,
for this was the way of
the merging of being,
and we were merged.

Our souls danced together
in the moment
ecstatic,
as if re-united
after a long separation,
each finding affirmation
in the other.

Our bodies moved to sound and music
not heard by human ears.

We floated in the spheres
forgetting our bodies,
the conditions of our physical birth,
and the learned restrictions
of our humanness.

And our beings, as two, became one again.

The sky supported us,
and as the sun set,
the rays of color surrounded us,
and we began to reflect
all color
within us,
forging a rainbow into our bodies.

We flew out of time and into space
where our union was completed,
for this is where it had begun.

The stars were at our fingertips
and danced between our hands
and shone from our eyes
and joined us in our merging.

The moon shone as a bright light upon us,
illuminating our path
through the heavens.

And we reached into light
and sent out the call
and were carried
on the wave
of creation.

There was no time,
no beginning and no end.

And the world faded,

A n d   W e   W e r e

H   O   M   E

BEING SEEN

I heard him pay Naomi for my services,
but what did he want? Why had he come to me?
For my time, my healing? Or, perhaps now, my wisdom.

Judas entered,
bowing his head to me as he crossed the threshold,
staring at me as if he had never seen me before.

And he said to me, "Magdalena, you are Christ's lover?"
And I said, "No."
He advanced toward me, grasping my arm, not roughly, but with
conviction. And he drew my fire unto him through his longing.
We looked into each other's eyes:
he, to discern the truth of my denial,
I to determine the reason for his presence.

He said, "You are the one. You are the one. I must learn it from you.
There is something that you must teach me, but I do not remember what
it is. I know that you are important to me, but I do not remember why."

He dropped my arm, and yet did not move away from me.
"You remain still," he said. "I know that you know the answers, and yet
you are still."

I said nothing, for there was nothing to say.
He must ask to receive, and so I waited.

213

The moment grew longer and the air thicker. He was torn, as we all were, between the flesh and the spirit, the human and the divine.

I waited as he searched my eyes, my face, for the answers.

"Tell me," he said, "please tell me. I must know."
"The keys to the kingdom are within," I said.
"Will you take me there?"
"Yes,"

He hesitated, as if he had expected me to reject him.
"Yes?" he repeated.
"Yes."

"I do not know what to do," he said. "I know in some way that it is different with you, but I do not know how."

He was perplexed—almost shy, somewhat tender, suddenly softer.

I smiled at him very gently, and he relaxed.

"I will show you. Breathe into my heart and look into my eyes," I said.

I began to draw him into me
slowly and gently
calling forth his essence,
that he would experience joy
in the merging.

214

I spoke to his soul and engaged it to power his journey.
I called in the lights, for this was the purpose of the joining.

I knew he would become my lover, had always known it,
because I remembered the design.
And once we had lain together, he would remember also.

There was nothing I had to do now. His body and soul were leading him.
His aura grew larger and began filling with light as the force of life
expanded within him and he experienced it fully. There was a surge of
energy between us, as the male and female polarities
caught and held.
I allowed my essence to flow into him.

This was his initiation, and I created the intention for it
to be a powerful one.

We moved together as one body now, each aware of the other and
yet not separated because of it.

He was strong and big and full of dichotomy.
A part of him was grave and questioning because of his role—
another part innocent and childlike, covered with a gruff aggressiveness.

I felt these layers dissolve and merge into a deep
peacefulness as we moved.
He relaxed because I did not challenge him.
So often challenged, he spent much of his energy warding it off.
And he did not need to here and was grateful.

215

He was aware of my guardedness also, and when I let it down, he
acknowledged that I had done so, his muscles loosening their tenseness
and his skin beginning to receive mine.
Our beings became fluid,
exchanging the current of passion
and compassion
which ran between us.

I began to do less and experience more,
for I was always the one to give.
And now, surprisingly,
he had something to give me,
and I allowed myself to receive it.

It was a new experience, a camaraderie,
a friendship—no struggle, no definition,
just being.

Our bodies continued to move
to a familiar rhythm, remembered, but never experienced.

This moment was a gift for us.
As players called to act,
we were dedicated to our mission,
humanly alone, not seen.

The gift of this joining was being seen—
Judas seeing me and knowing me and accepting me,
and I him.

It delighted me.
An openness and playfulness infused our passion.
There were no taboos, no rules, no overlays.
I was truly free with this man.
Now I had no more responsibility to his soul, for unlike the others,
his soul was actualized, now working according to the plan.

I had never lain with a man and known such a total
physical merging.
He touched places within me
which brought me pleasure
and joy
and a longing to be ordinary
and to forget the design.

And as we merged,
an unspoken agreement was forged between
our bodies and our souls,
that we would give each other this gift
many, many times,
and create from our union a space of peace
in the never-ending design
of the resurrection.

THE BALANCE OF POWER

I sent out the call to Christ one week after I lay with Judas. My thoughts and feelings were confused, for there were now two men in my heart and I knew I must speak of it to him. Although I knew the design, I worried that he would be angry. My love for him had not changed, and yet I was the same no longer.

He was in Capernaum making connection with the holy men there, laying the groundwork for a healing station, and it took him four days to return.

I knew that my laying with Judas would stir his resolve to complete his calling. I had not lain with Judas to hurt him, and he would know this. And yet his initial response could be anger, only, I guessed, because we could not lay together, not because he begrudged Judas and me the union.

He would go away and be alone, and as a result, forge with the power of his knowing. Opening up the channels of force within him, he would command the fields of energy and gravity, speaking to them of his need and changing their patterning. He would come to understand the force fields of creation, walking on water, raising the dead, and healing the dying, and the people would speak of him, after he had gone, as the creator of heaven on Earth.

I helped him to integrate the memory of the knowledge within his soul and guided him in his unfolding, but there were still pathways he had to learn, and he had to learn them alone, as we all do.

He had to learn what it is to be truly alone humanly and to acknowledge the memory of one's calling completely.

Often, he had been so preoccupied with his mission that he was unaware of what was around him. This must change or he could not lead. His preoccupation must shift to an all-seeing vision. Alone in the desert he would forge it, and then we would truly begin.

We stood without words when he arrived. He was concerned, afraid something had happened. He was not centered in himself, and so I drew him to me before he could speak, and we breathed together to calm us.

I looked into his eyes and said, "I love you, my husband." And I meant: the one who shares my deepest life. There came to his eyes a look of undeniable panic.

"You say that with finality. What are you saying? I know we are always to be together. . . forever. What is it?"

"Do you remember your lessons?" I asked.

He became angry at me. "My lessons? What do my lessons have to do with this?"

"I ask because it is important."

"I want to balance the power," he said.

"I give my permission." It was the first time he had challenged me, asking that we have equal say in what we created together.

So we sat with legs crossed on the floor facing each other. He placed his hand on my heart, and I placed my hand on his heart. We closed our eyes, and our fears crystallized in front of us: our fear of failing to accomplish our mission, our fear of aloneness, and the fear of separation from God, our selves, and each other. We acknowledged the fears, sending the love back and forth to the other's heart. We did so as an affirmation of our complete union, knowing that a struggle for power would serve no purpose, and trusting enough to love completely. We were one essence then, our conscious union allowing us to know our oneness more completely. We were equal and strong and fully open to each other, completely together, and the fears dissolved.

"I am now ready to see it," he said.

I breathed deeply, and remembering my merging with Judas, played the vision through my awareness without words. I left nothing out, because I could not. An essence is an essence, and therefore, imparts itself completely.

And he saw it.

All I could do in that moment was to keep my heart totally open to him. I waited, watching the images playing across his consciousness.

When he spoke, his voice was detached, and he spoke not of what he had seen.

"I must go away."

"I know."

He changed his focus again, saying, "Your heart is so open to me, and now to him. It is a tribute."

"Yes," I said, "a tribute to you and to our love and to our union."

He was quiet for a moment and then he said, "You know that I wish it had been me?"

"Yes," I said. "And you know that I wish it had been also, with all my heart."

He nodded. "Tell me."

I settled myself and began to tell him how it was. "I knew that he would come, because I remembered who he is. What was a surprise, was the understanding I felt from him. He knew me, mortally, as no other person has: not my mother, my father, my sisters, my friends, my women, the men. He knew me without words and gave me of himself, allowing himself to trust me," I said.

"Yes, the trust. . . always the trust," Christ said. "There is a part of me that feels betrayed, you know." I felt the current of anger run through him. "Is there anything that you do not know?" he asked, unexpectedly. He smiled, an incongruous movement of his lips.

"You know what I gave him?" I asked.

"Yes," he answered. "I know it was necessary and right, and I do not begrudge you or him the pleasure of the merging.
I am glad that you have him, for I must go away."

"You do know that this will make it easier for you to go," I said.

He seemed about to laugh and caught himself, saying, "Ah, the design!"

"It angers me, too, at times," I said. "When I was with Judas. . . do you not understand? It was as if we escaped it for a time, could live and love outside of the knowledge somehow."

"Oh, how I wish for the same opportunity!" He stopped a moment, seemed ready to go on, and then said, "Wait now! If this has happened for you, this gift, it is a part of the design. You have created this, both of you, to make it easier for you. If you both decided to do this, what is to say that you and I. . ." He did not finish his sentence. It was almost as if he could not.

"Look for me, my Mary. I am too close to it to see it. Is there a way?"

I knew what he was asking and that he was serious, and my breath caught. It was unthinkable, and yet. . . I remembered the ones with no names saying, "Ask and you shall receive. There is no right and wrong, only divine truth."

I breathed and relaxed as much as I could and sent my thoughts away, freeing my link to the pathways.

I opened my awareness to speak with the ones with no names and asked them to show me the design.

I knew they would show me the reality called parallel so that I could see and weigh the options and choose the outcome, seeing the consequences of the actions we would choose to take.

They showed me the four realities: the actual, potential, probable, and possible. I saw our pattern and followed it through all the way, looking at each aspect and all the choices we could make. I knew that the design must stay complete, and any change we made must not affect the final outcome.

And the design held and I breathed, and I did it all again, twice more to be sure, and I could feel him waiting, almost without breath, for my answer. And still I hesitated. It was a great risk. I would need to direct my passion and his without faltering, raising our life force into union. I sighed.

Then softly, in my awareness, there was a voice, familiar. . . a lullaby remembered. "It is what you do best," came the words. And the tension eased, and I laughed silently at myself that I had been afraid. There is never anything to fear. I would not have been shown the realities if I had not had the ability to use them effectively. It was all a part of the divine order.

I was taking too long, and Christ stirred beside me. "Well, what did they say?" he asked.

"They said, 'yes!'" I said, smiling.

We were aware of a heightened perception suddenly, as if the room were hotter. His breathing had changed.

"You are blushing," he said, and I lowered my eyes.

"What is it?" he asked. We were still facing each other, with our hands resting on each other's heart. I was suddenly shy, feeling what was to come, and I withdrew my hand to calm myself.

He said suddenly and insistently, "Do not leave, my Mary, nothing is worth your leaving."

I gave him my hand again, coming back to myself and to him. Then I spoke, telling him of what I had seen.

"You are to plant your seed inside no woman," I said distinctly, "and no woman is to touch you in a sexual way," I paused.

"Yes, and . . . ?" he prodded.

"The lights were showing me an alternative," I said and blushed deeply again. "It would help me if you would look for yourself!" I said, only half teasing.

So he did, and the color deepened in his cheeks also. When he looked again at me, his eyes were very bright.

He said, "You will whisper the words of passion into my ears?"

"Yes," I said.

"And you will raise the fire within us, and we will feel our unity in every physical cell?"

"Yes."

"And we will lie one next to the other and I will know, almost, what it
is like?"

"You will know exactly if you expand your consciousness," I answered.
"Remember, there is no separation. It will be as in the waterfall, and yet
more physical, for we will stay in our bodies. And then you will know how
it is. It will be a moment when you realize your full humanity and, at the
same moment, your full union with God."

"And for you? Will it be the same for you? I mean. . ."

He was blushing again, and yet, persisted. "It will be as such for you?"

I breathed in his question and the love which had birthed it, and I knew
in that moment my deepest joy. To know this man was the greatest gift of
my life. To love him completely, as they now said was possible, was to be
filled to overflowing with the sweetest nectar of the Earth and beyond.
I had no words. His question was born of inexperience and nervousness. I
was even now feeling our merging in my body, knowing its sweetness.

He was shy, waiting for my answer. Then suddenly, he breathed into me
and felt my thoughts and knew them, and he smiled, and we began.

"What else is there you need to tell me?" he asked.

He was reading my mind, and I teased him about it. We were as two lovers
playing before the energy rises to align with the dance of the bodies.

"I saw that this will bring you fully into your field of power. You will need to be in your body completely in the desert to survive."

"How did you know I will go?" he asked, as if he did not know the answer. "How did you know I would really choose to go?"

"I have been watching the design for many days. I knew you would go and that you will feel anger against me at times, and it saddens me."

"Perhaps I will, later." He paused. "Now, in this moment, be with me. Show me the pathway to mortal pleasure. It is the least you can do," he added.

And I knew he joked with me, for his heart was open.

"It is quite a responsibility," I said.

"No, no—You are the one who has the ability to respond, that is all."

"Damn you for all that knowledge," I joked, "I am only human, after all."

"As am I," he responded.

Our eyes caught and held, and the music began, carrying us into our senses fully.

And the arc of our covenant manifested in the form we had seen in our vision, and we were aware only of each other and the energy which exploded inside our bodies.

I felt the enormity of the moment and what was transferred, and I gave him my feminine energy and power freely.

And the pendulum swung

female into male

and we were one.

And the most incredible revelation was that it was a

part of the design.

By asking, we had received.

THE SERMON ON THE MOUNT

I was walking in the desert,
following Christ and
leading him at the same time.

My feet ached with the heat
and the distance.
It seemed so far, so far,
as if we had walked forever.

The mountains shimmered in the heat of the day,
beacons of power surrounding us,
beckoning us to hurry.

We knew the importance of this moment in time.
Much rested on it.
The future, as humans would know it,
rested on this moment.

It was his first sermon and would address all the people,
all of them, and give them faith.
They would follow him in earnest,
and all the prophecies would then be true,
for he would fulfill them.

He was not feeling ready,
did not know what he would say.

And yet I knew the words,
for I could reach into the future
and hear them as yet unspoken,
forming on the brink of eternity
and resounding throughout the
halls of time.

They were a part of the records called
the Sermon on the Mount—
a turning point for all the people.

Nothing would be the same again.

And as we walked,
the Earth crumbled and gave way under our feet,
as if knowing it must move
and yield to the new way.

I was in my body and his at the same time.
I felt the leanness of him, the caring,
and yet the ambivalence.
I knew his thoughts, his fears, his misgivings.
He did not feel ready.

The mission was clear, the delivery uncertain.

And we walked as if through time
> to find the path
> to the word
> which would manifest the truth
> into this time and place.

I began to project the words onto his consciousness
to form a bridge with the people
and the words
and the dance
> > which would bring them home.

We merged as we walked, as if we were alone.
The people were waiting and following at the same time,
and yet, we were alone, he and I.

The forces of all time and space merged into the unity of
this moment with us.
And the people felt it, and began to crowd around us as we walked.

The heat was rising up from the land

> > and called out as a force.

The sun formed rays of orange light upon our
chests and bodies
and brought forth a steadiness, as if

> > drawing us into the flame.

And so we walked, miles and miles it seemed.

235

I stayed within the hologram of time,
seeing all the points
and not belonging to any of them.

And I was h e
              and I was m e
                          and I was n e i t h e r.

The people walked between us. Christ took the lead as we walked, and I stayed behind. When we came to the mountain he stopped, suddenly sensing the place of power from which he would speak.

I saw a shudder run through his body, and then he straightened himself, planting his feet firmly on the ground. He stood for some moments with his back to us, drawing the substance of the ethers through his body and into the core of the Earth.

The people felt his presence growing, and they stopped walking.
They waited in silence.

Christ turned to face the people, and they began to settle themselves into the hillside at the base of the mountain, sitting on the ground at his feet.

I felt the angels and the beings of light descend to him. The kingdoms lent to him their power and their presence through the fiber of being.
A magnitude grew around him, and the people felt it. They prepared to listen, knowing before he began the importance of this moment.

The light which he brought was pure, clear, wise, and all-seeing.

In the desert he had unified with his knowing and now he stood before the people, whole—love streaming from his heart, his soul shining the light of its becoming onto the Earth.

They awaited grace.   They longed for divinity.

In human form he would speak to them as the son of God,
telling them that they were the same as he.

And I rejoiced that it was so.

The wind gusted around us suddenly, and as he began to speak, the trees rustled their leaves in accordance.
The elements rejoiced, for his words were an acknowledgment of the wisdom now to be at one with the people.

He lifted his arms and spoke slowly and distinctly, with power and eloquence. His voice echoed within the hallowedness of the mountains, and peace settled into the valley around him.

"And so, my people, what is it to be spirit in flesh?" he paused, "and how have we come to be here?"

He stopped speaking, his questions alive in the air around us as the words echoed forth from the mountains.

There was an expectant hush, and the people leaned forward as he began to speak again. He looked at them, each one, drawing from them the flame of truth within and joining it with his own. They felt at one with him then, trusting his words and his intention.

"It is as this," he continued:

In the flesh is the longing for life and death
at the same moment, unresolved!

In the flesh is the longing for freedom and the need of security
at the same moment, unresolved!

In the flesh is sorrow for the grief of our mothers who carry us from light into darkness and know not how to return us to light again!

In the flesh is the pain of our fathers who know we cannot find our souls—the pain of knowing they have given their power to the elders, elders who tell them they have lost their souls because they have sinned!

In the flesh is the search for the meaning of love and trust and union, in a world of hatred, jealousy and separation.

This then is the meeting place of flesh and spirit! The promise and the living so different, and yet—

Are we not the spirit in flesh? Is it not the knowledge of this which compels us to search? Is it not our soul which brings the light from the darkness of the world, to sit beside us and guide us onward, giving us solace? Is it not the soul which urges us to kindness and speaks to us of love?

There is no separation, for within you in the seed of your soul is the unity and truth which you seek. It does not exist outside of you, in the world. It exists within you.

Within you is the death and the birth, the light and the dark, the peace and the power. The soul and the knowledge within you are the meeting place of spirit and flesh, the oneness that you seek!

Where there is one soul, there is the kingdom of heaven!

You have come a great distance from the house of the Father and Mother, and you seek here for the truth and knowledge that exists there, in the kingdom of the Gods.

And I say to you that the Father and the Mother and all of the Gods have placed within you their kingdom! For you are here to create that kingdom in this place of Earth.

Know that the light of the world is within you and carries the code of survival for all people, for all life!

In the darkness of the night is the light of the world visible through your choices and your actions.
Let your light so shine among men that they will know your Father and Mother who are in heaven!

Yours is the mission of peace, my people.

Yours is the mission of love, my people.

Search no more!

Long no more!

What you seek the Gods have given you.
Claim, each of you, the right to the divinity of your birth.

Give to no one the power to rule your heart, for the knowledge of the Lord and the Goddess is within you and saith:

Fear not for I am with you.
My rod and my staff, they comfort you.
We preparest a table before you
in the presence of thine enemies. . . .
Surely goodness and mercy
shall follow you
all the days of your life
and you will dwell in the house of the Lord
forever. He paused.
"Where is the house of the Lord?
Where is the kingdom of heaven?"

He looked at them, a smile lingering at the corners of his lips.
His love was a force reaching out and gathering them within his bosom,
and as I watched, he rocked them and soothed them and brought them
home.

And then he spoke once more.

The time is at hand—
the kingdom of heaven is within.

We, together, are the kingdom of heaven.
You and I and all of the people.
The kingdom of heaven is not with our Father and Mother above.
It is with us here, below!

We are born of the light!
We carry the light!
We are the light!
The light is within us!

Let your light so shine before men
that the people may know of the truth
because you are!

Blessed are you that shine light on the darkness
of the world, for you will find the kingdom of heaven.

I watched as the people gathered around him, opening unto him, receiving from him, loving him. And I knew we had done well, knew that all the prophesies had been fulfilled, and that the union we had seen would come to pass. My heart overflowed with joy, and I gave thanks.

AT ONE WITH THE KINGDOMS

The blooming flowers of my garden surrounded us in scent as we lay together on the rich softness of the summer grass. The branches of the olive trees covered us in shade, yielding us protection from the fierceness of the sun's calling. It was midday, and Christ and I had talked for many hours of Israel, of the people, and of the future.

We knew we were leaving here and wondered what the years ahead would bring to this sacred land. Would the people honor Israel after the resurrection and the years of searching and unrest which would follow? There would be a time when we knew they would forget who they were.

We knew that part of our calling was to teach them of the fiber of being: their oneness with each other, the land, and the kingdoms, so that they could choose to remember it. But would they ultimately choose to remember? Would they choose to honor the sacredness of this land?

I leaned over him, looking at him as he lay beside me. There were lines now on his face, around his eyes, springing from the edges of his mouth. I traced them with my finger. I remembered when we were young, only beginning to know the importance of our calling. I felt in these lines the days and years of our learning, and I felt a great tenderness for him.

When I had first seen him I was six years, and our families were passing the Sabbath together. He was two years, and his legs were so short they could barely carry his body. He had just begun to speak, and at the end of the day, when it was time for the leaving, Elisabeth and Miriamne had brought him to me and he held out his tiny hand and said, "My Mar-eee."

Then I remembered the first time we had gone walking into the trees together and found the fairies and danced with them. It was when we were children still, before our time at the Sea of Galilee.
He looked up at me then, asking me with his mind where my thoughts were going. I told him, asking him if he remembered the day when we had gone to be with the little people, and they had let us join in their celebration.

As an answer, he projected the images of us as children onto my mind.

When I saw the images, I remembered that special day, and I rolled onto
my back and closed my eyes, watching as he led me through the
memory of us

playing and dancing

in the trees beyond my father's house.

We began to run, and the joy in our oneness led us into the hills.
We danced with the Earth and the sky
and called the devas, those that represent the nature kingdoms,
to join us.

They answered our calling and showed us their images, projecting them onto
our minds as form. They were small, three feet high, and stocky.
The women wore crowns made from the boughs of trees. Their dresses were
beautiful and had sashes with pictures of animals and flowers and suns and
moons upon them.

The men wore large hats and shirts of bright colors. They brought flowers to
the circle for a ritual of fertility and danced in tribute to the Earth, thanking
her for giving them food for the winter and praying to her for the seeds they
would plant in the spring.
After a time they motioned for us to join them inside their circle, and they
made a ceremony of light for us.

It was an initiation.

They united us with the forces of nature:
the kingdoms of rocks and minerals and plants and animals,
and the elements of wind and sky and sea and sun and moon,
and we were well-honored.

They spoke to us through their minds of the bond between man and nature,
instructing us in the ways of joining with them.

They showed us that if you ask, a rock will hold out its arm to give strength,
the ocean will carry power to you as the wave comes to shore,
the wind will give you your direction, and the old trees will tell you the places
of safety, water, and shelter. They led us through all the elements, one by one,
showing us what each one would share with us if we honored it and asked.

There was a time to come in the design when we would call the forces of
nature to join with us, and we knew we had made a bond between humans
and fairies and kingdoms and elements which would stand throughout time.

Our people would always have the choice to work with nature, and the
connection could never be broken because the current which runs as the force
of life in all species unites all life as one.

We knew this because it is a part of the
design of order that all kingdoms are one,
now and always.
We listened and remembered
and joyfully began to sing and dance with them.

When we had feasted and danced,
we sat and talked, dreaming with them of the ways
of all beings.
Our life forces merged with theirs,
and we knew their way and their truth,
and they knew ours.

Then we all linked our arms
and slept
as the stars rose to join us
in the dark sky of night.

As Christ and I remembered the vows we had made as children, we again pledged our love and support in bringing together the people with the land, the elements, and the nature spirits. He held me close as the day grew older, and we spoke of what we had accorded with the fairies and the kingdoms. We wondered what we could do to assure the memory of the people about their oneness with all life.

What we realized finally, after hours of discussion, was that humans would know their connection to the kingdoms and the elements only through the connection with themselves and the seed of light within their soul—would know oneness with all life only from acknowledging the light within them, the light which is within all life.

And so we affirmed again our calling to the soul, for herein lay the pathway to the preservation of the Earth and her kingdoms.

THE ROMAN

The city was alive with color and delight, its busy streets lined with carts and wagons, animals and children, all jostling each other as they moved. I loved the bustle and the life. I walked behind the vendors, enjoying the day, observing the activity. People crowded around the wares, bargaining and haggling over each piece with mock ferociousness. There was banter and rejoicing, for the long heat of the summer was over. The crispness of the fall air was felt in the dancing leaves, and the people were happy, shouting and teasing.

The women wore gaily colored scarves in celebration, and as they bought the foods and wares, they stayed together, chattering about their goods and bragging about their bargains.

Even the Romans seemed in good spirits this day, leaving the people to their celebrations. They leaned in the archways watching the women, joking among themselves and jesting as they drank their ale.

I glanced at them as I passed, careful not to invite conversation or acknowledgment, for the soldiers were known to taunt and tease and rape the women of my people, and so they were not to be trusted. I had no personal fear of them, but I knew their ways and did not challenge them or give them cause to challenge me.

I looked up, surprising a Roman soldier who stood staring at me. He did not look away, although he seemed uncertain. For some reason, I did not look away either, and we stood for a moment, openly acknowledging the other. He appeared to know who I was, for I saw recognition in his eyes, and yet we had never spoken before.

I knew the Romans watched me and that I was a mystery to them. But they had never found fault with me or my attitude toward them, and so they left me alone.

Perhaps he knew me by reputation. Yet there was no suspicion in his eyes, only recognition, and a question. Yes. A question which now seemed to draw me to him.

I walked toward him, and we realized at the same moment that we could not speak here on the street. Our people were enemies, and there was no reason for us to speak, no reason for us to pursue friendship.

I asked myself what I was doing. Why was I going toward him?
I had no answer, but I knew then that we would talk and that it was important and had something to do with the design.

254

I nodded to him slightly, moving quickly away from him and the soldiers nearby. I walked without looking back, pacing my steps so that he could follow me if he wished to.

I lingered in the marketplace, touching some wares and purchasing a purple and gold covering for my hair. I looked behind me as I moved down the street, but he did not follow me, so I continued with my shopping and returned home.

Late that afternoon, I heard the festivities in the city below, the people becoming gayer and the noise growing louder as night approached.

Naomi was away in the town buying the food for our dinner, and so when he knocked at the door, it was I who answered.

He had removed his soldier's cloths and wore a tunic of soft ruby color. I would not have known he was a Roman. He was handsome to me, tall and broad, with brown hair and a gentle smile which played at the corners of his eyes and lips. He smiled at me with a recognition that I felt as well, but was more hesitant to acknowledge.

He spoke first: "You are the one of Migdala, called Mary Magdalena?"

"Yes." I waited, offering no more information.

"I have come because there is a matter we must discuss. Will you speak with me now?"

He looked past me through the door, as if making certain that I was alone so that we could speak unobserved.

"Yes, I will talk with you," I said, moving aside as he entered my home. I covered the window by the door as a sign to Naomi that I was not alone.

He studied me openly and honestly, without pretense. I did not invite him to sit, and we stood, feeling an urgency suddenly upon us.

"I lead the Roman army, Mary," he said suddenly. "The soldiers take their orders from me."

A shiver went through my body. "And why are you here?" I asked, sensing the answer before he said it.

"I am here because of him."

"Oh," I said, sitting down. I felt a sudden chill in the air and knew the chill was from my heart.

"I thought you would know who I am," he said to me.

"I have been watching you now for many months, hoping you would come and speak to me of the matters to which we must both attend." He paused, "And when you did not, I decided to take matters into my own hands. You know what I must do, and we must talk. You must meet me at my place of living tonight. I cannot stay here, for your safety, as you must know."

He gave me the direction, we set the hour, and he was gone.

I sat for several hours as the damp coldness of the day spread through my home and into my bones, and I saw then what I had not seen before. I saw the plan and the agreement and the design of what must happen, step by step.

I bathed and ate and brought out my black tunic and shawl. After the moon had made her way across the sky, I made my way to his place of living. I went slowly and carefully, remaining in the shadows when necessary, assuring that I was not seen. It took me a long time, for we lived at opposite ends of the great city; I to the east and he to the west.

His place of living was set apart from the other Romans, and he was waiting for me, opening the door and guiding me inside as I came to the door frame. His living quarters were luxurious, the walls and floors lined with furs and appointed with gold, a bright fire burning on the hearth. There was wealth here, opulence.

As I looked around, my eyes took in the brightness of the room, and I wondered at my boldness in coming here and my trust in the design. I breathed to calm myself and to feel my power fully.

He must have read my thoughts, for he said, "Mary of Migdala, you know that you are safe here with me."

"Yes," I said.

"Here now, come and sit and I will give you wine. Wrap this fur around your shoulders, and we will begin," he said to me, his big hand on my shoulder, holding out for me a beautiful black fur.

I did as he bid, for it would feel good to be warm and to drink and to sit after my long journey.

He poured wine, and as I drank he stared at me without pretense. I was aware again of his honesty. Here was a man, a Roman, I could trust.

I felt his kindness, and I knew it had been difficult for him to approach me, so I began the conversation.

"After you left this day, I began to view the records and to remember what we have agreed to do. I now understand your place in the design and will accord it. I honor your knowing and am grateful that you came to me so that we may prepare."

He said nothing for some moments, staring into the smoldering fire.

When he spoke again, he did not look at me.

"I thank you for the accordance and for your honoring. I know some of what is to come, but I do not see it all. That is why I came to you. I find myself with visions of what I know to be the future, and yet they are incomplete visions, images that are unreal. They are smudged at the edges. So many with free will. I sometimes wonder if I know anything at all." He stopped suddenly, confused and frustrated.

He looked at me then and said, "Mary, I hope that you can help me to see the design, for I know the part I play, we play, is important, and we must honor what has been pre-ordained. It is such a curse to me sometimes.

"Why I agreed to do this eludes me. I am a sworn officer of the Roman empire, and yet I am ready to aid Christ to escape death at the hands of my own army."

I was moved by his searching and his questions. We had all asked questions such as these many times, and I knew this was the first time that he could voice them. I suddenly felt his aloneness more profoundly than my own, and gave thanks to the lights that I could share my life with so many others. This man was truly alone, and my heart went out to him.

"Come sit beside me," I said, "and I will lead you through the pathways."

There was something in my voice, he told me later, which gave him solace. He knew that whatever I would do would bring him peace, so he rose from his place across from me and came to sit beside me.

I took his left hand between my two hands and closed my eyes. I sent out the call to the lights to surround us as we journeyed and began to merge my energy with his as we sat together. Immediately, we moved through time and space, and the future began to play in front of us. At first we saw the other afresh, seeing this meeting and then our talks as they deepened and other meetings that would be necessary to create the design. We saw the end as clearly as the beginning; and when we were through we sat with no words spoken, absorbing the visions and the truths, silently acknowledging to each other who we were and what we had come to do.

It was he who broke the silence. "I have been totally alone my whole life. I have traveled the world as we know it, seen the good and the bad as we live it, and have searched for some way to explain it.

And then, two years ago, I began to see these visions that we have just seen, as I said, in fragments, never this completely. I am very grateful to you for showing me these truths, for I have judged my actions and have torn myself asunder trying to understand what would move me to act in the ways I have seen. Now I know why, and that, at least, is a blessing. Thank you."

Before I could reply, he withdrew his hand and was up again, tending to the fire, refilling my wine glass, and resuming his place across from me.

He seemed unsettled.

"What is it?" I asked him.

"You do not know? I will betray my country. I will betray my people. It is so much."

I waited a moment before replying, feeling how fully the weight of the actions we had seen played upon his conscience. "Yes, perhaps. But you are of all people, and you will not betray your God or Christ. You will know that in the accordance of the design is the salvation of all people. Remember—you are not a man of the world; you are a man of God."

He did not answer me directly, but said, "I know that you face the same dragons. How do you live with the people and the questions and the reality and the illusion? Sometimes it is so unclear to me, and I have had no one to talk with about it. There is no one but you. I trust no one else, ultimately, and I trust you only because I have been shown your face in my dreams for as long as I can remember.

"When I first saw you on the street, my men were pointing at you and saying that you were the one who was always with Christ and that you were under suspicion with him. That is when the visions started, and I watched you and tried to put it together, but the pieces never fit before."

He stopped suddenly and looked at me again from across the room. "And now, of course, all the pieces fit, for I know who you are."

I inclined my head to him, for I knew what he meant and knew the relief it brought.

Then he said, "You are to me the most beautiful woman I have ever seen. I war with myself not only about my part in the design but also about my part in your future. What is your place in the life of Christ? What is your calling? May I ask you these questions, and will you answer freely?"

He fascinated me. Every time that I thought I knew how he thought and where he was, he would turn to another part of himself and surprise me.

"I would be glad to speak to you of my life," I said, "for I know that you and I are to live the design as friends, and you will be with me many times in this turning.

"Christ is my greatest friend, my greatest love.
We are the same soul in two forms: female and male.
There is a bond between us that cannot be broken and calls forth unity from every part of our being. He is as I, and I am as he.

"I have come here to remember the design and to lead my people through Christ, and then, ultimately, he will lead them through me for we are the same. Since the life has been of the woman's calling for thousands of years, I and my sisters have come to teach him and to guide him in the ways of power and to pass to him the torch of guardianship. He will be the guardian for the next two thousand years when we will again be born to right the balance of power, and the male and female will create equally. I am his counterpart, his teacher, and his friend; I am not his lover. He is to have no physical lover in this life as Christ, for it is not of his highest calling. I, however, do not have the same calling. I am free to be with anyone I choose. I am free to love fully, without constraint."

I paused for a moment, thinking, and then continued, "He and I work with the people, touching their bodies and healing them. We help them to remember that they are one with the Gods and that they are not alone. They are vulnerable, seeking a truth that we know and can accord them, and therefore we do not deal with them as we would a partner in the design. It is a point of honor for us, and so we stay separate—in a sense, unseen. Unseen, that is, with the exception of Judas." I paused, long enough for the Roman to know what I would say next.

"You love Judas?" he asked.

"Yes, of course I love him. He is one of us and also remembers the design."

He made a sound deep in his throat, and I realized that he meant, was I in love with Judas?

"Yes, I am in love with Judas. Our love is physical and sensual, and we find respite together from the design. Our love affords us companionship and brings us solace."

"You bring me solace, also, Mary."

I looked at him and chose to remain silent. I did not know what he would say next. I felt him, had been feeling him for hours at the edges of my body. There was a starburst of desire in my center which came and went. I was aware of the passion which flowed between us; it ebbed as we would start to discover a piece of the puzzle, or to put another piece in place and then the passion returned again to flow between us.

I knew we both held it off, talking of the design and each other and what we had created in our lives. And why I did not know, for there was no reason for us to hold it off, no reason on Earth. We lived outside of the rules and customs of the people, free to be alive in ways that they judged and condemned. So why did we hold it off?

"For me," he said, answering my unspoken question, "there is a reluctance to share myself with you too quickly. I want to savor this, Mary. I want to know you completely, and I want you to have a place in my life. And you cannot have a place in my life. We will meet infrequently, always in secret, and then it will be the turning and you will be gone, and I will be the one who assures it. I would laugh at the ironies if I did not feel so angry and alone. In some ways you are my only guard against aloneness.

"I have seen no other woman's face in my dreams. No one else has found her way into my heart. There is no one else, and yet, I do not even know you."

He paused, "It is so confusing. I am decisive and commanding, yet about this I know nothing. I must defer to a greater wisdom."

He looked at me imploringly, and then he rose and placed more wood on the fire. He poured us both wine, and returned to his place across the room. He kept his distance, and yet I felt him beside me, felt him within me, already in my heart and in my flesh.

I closed my eyes, the furs and the warmth and the wine blurring the moment. I went inside to think, to retreat, to relax, and to ask for guidance.

And what the ones with no names said did not surprise me: what we did was for our conscience to decide, and all that they wished for us was joy. And the joy was in this moment, not in the next, not tomorrow and in all the tomorrows of our aloneness.
It was now.
The joy was now.
His concerns were of the structure and the form and not of the being; therefore they would pass, and what we would have is what we created, in this moment.

He called my name softly, yet I did not stir. He thought me to be asleep, and so he rose and came beside me, touching my face with his longing.

I felt this caress upon my cheeks, and I opened my eyes as if his hand had touched me.

He held back, as if going forward would take from him the truth of what we had, rather than making it real.

I looked at him with my heart in my eyes and waited. I spoke no words to convince him or deter him, did not share with him what the voices had said to me. I simply allowed the moment to speak of itself.

And very slowly he received the knowing of the moment, and I watched it ease the questions and the searching. I watched his brow relax.

I knew then that he would lay with me, for now would be the only time in his vision that the loneliness would cease to exist.
Now was all that he had.

He was still reluctant to touch me, holding it off, and yet I knew it would be good and rich and slow, for he savored me, even now. I laughed suddenly, the joy catching fire in my heart, and I reached out my arms to him, and he came into them and lifted me in one motion. And what I remember was the soft warmth of the furs, the hardness of his body, and the gentleness with which he took me home.

THE LIGHT AND DARK IN MY HEART

Sitting by the window in my home on the Mount of Olives, I looked out onto the garden of Gethsemane. The midday shadows made patterns of light and dark on the trees and the Earth. I sat watching, thinking of the dream I had last night—a dream about my future, my choices, and the outcome of those choices. It brought me to the awareness of how important choice is, and as I thought of my choices, I looked into my future.

More clearly than ever, the patterns of my life changed and moved, as did the shadows before me in my garden. I felt these same shadows within me as well, sometimes brighter, sometimes darker, opening the pathways of my heart. As I felt my heart open, I saw the future stretch before me as a long hallway, with doors on either side. At each door was a person and a path and a destiny. They were all there, each of the players.

I saw the people whom I loved so dearly: my mother, the Mother of Christ, and then Elisabeth. I felt the ease of the love between us, the bonds of sisterhood, and the fragrance of womanness.

Then I saw Christ, and the joy of him filled my heart, as I remembered all our times of union.

The future showed us leaving Israel after the resurrection with Judas and Thomas. The four of us would share the danger and the drama, wound together in union through the journey.

It would take a long time, the passage from Israel to safety, and even then our safety would be relative, for some would know whence we had come. We would be guarded by those who understood the design, living quietly, silently moving from place to place, meeting only those we were guided to trust, those who bore the sign of the fish, the sign of the one. It is one thing to run and hide, and another to know that you are safe, and I saw that we would know both at the same time. And so we would live, our sanity assured only through this knowing.

Thomas would leave us in the Grecian islands, and then the three of us would hold tightly together, making our way through new lands to France. I saw Christ, weakened from the ordeal in Israel, needing love and support during our long journey. He would rest for a time and we would make a home together until he was ready to travel and teach. I felt unconditional love with Christ, saw his leaving and our reunion many years in the future after I had left Judas.

Judas. I stopped at the door where he stood. He came from the door frame, and in my vision, we walked into the future together. I saw us as friends first and lovers second. Then I saw us as man and woman, living together as I had with no man, in the way of the flesh and the heart, bearing to him the fruits of union, bringing forth three souls whom we would raise together, two boys and one girl.

Traveling from place to place, we would heal and teach, building and sustaining, one to the other, content to live in holy marriage, the union of male and female.

Always more to see, more to be, one to the other, we would discover our humanness, enjoying our bodies, gathering our spirits in oneness. And yet the shadows were there with him, shadows that were there with no other except my sister Martha.

Martha entered my mind and I saw them together. They did not come apart as with a normal thought, ideas streaming in and out, they stayed together, and because of this I saw the future. I saw her finding us in France, weaving her pattern of deception and seduction.
The seeing brought pain to my heart, but I stayed with the design, knowing that I must see the outcome to know the truth.

I would find her lying with Judas, and I would finish that turning to begin yet another, leaving them together and being alone.

I saw my parting with Judas and the thirty years of journey to find Christ, to help him teach and heal and then die. The records showed that I would help his passing and then find my own passing in the place of Tibet.

As I sat, the years and the miles yet to come were heavy in my heart, as was the grief.

I saw my life divided into three turnings, and I was but living the first. This first turning would end this year with the resurrection.

So much yet to live and learn.

I sighed, my heart confused from the memory of what was yet to come. The patterns of the sun in the garden reflected the patterns of life in my heart: bright and dark, standing not still, always moving with each of the players.

I knew I could not judge the bright as better than the dark, could not defend myself from the future or change the past, but I must live only in the moment, for that was all I had.

Naomi came to my side gently, offering me some brew, and I thanked her and drank of its warmth. I felt it soothe me, as was her intention, and I smiled at the kindness of her caring.

The shadows still played on the garden and within my heart, and I looked again at the hallway of time. The Roman came to stand at his door frame then, and we walked together into the future.

When we had come together, that first time in his home, it was tender and the passion flowed easily. The way of the merging was deep and peaceful as still water, and we discovered within its depths the joy of desire, acceptance, and peace.

As it came time for us to effect the design, we met several times alone, and then with Christ and Judas, and then with Joseph of Arimathea.

Each time the Roman was afraid for me, for all of us, and we spoke in a heated way, for he wished to change the design. And so we ran it through the pathways again and again, and we came away knowing that we must uphold what the records showed us.

I reassured him over and over, but even now, as we made the final preparations with Joseph, he was unsure.

As he met me in the pathway of my heart, I saw our parting:

We stood together in the cave on the hillside near my garden, holding each other. Our hearts were one heart, woven through our longing, our love, and our sadness. As our tears flowed from our grieving, we expanded together and the design showed us the resolution of grieving— each of us one day finding the union we sought.

Then the records showed me what else he had come to learn: to trust in the unseen, in the design, and in the Gods; to know that he was a man of all people; and as with Judas, to remember that there is no betrayal—that we all create the reality we experience. We know always all that transpires, even when our mind would deny such, and speak otherwise. We were all here to learn that there is no betrayal: the Roman would not betray his people, Judas would not betray Christ, and Martha would not betray me. We were here to learn and to teach each other to trust.

The irony of this knowing shook the shadows on the surface of my heart, bringing to me a clarity I had not known before, and I gave thanks.

Then the shadows cleared, and there was the image of one who would not need to learn of trust—Joseph of Arimathea, our dear friend.

I was very small when first we met. One fine spring day the Mother of Christ took me by the hand and walked me to his home. She said she was taking me to meet a very good friend and that she would leave me with him for a time, returning at dark to sup together with us.

273

This man, called Joseph of Arimathea, was very kind to me. He gave me sweet figs and showed me his animals which roamed on the hillsides surrounding his home. We walked together over his land and through his gardens and sat beneath the olive trees talking.

He was kinder to me than any other man I had met. He listened to me as if what I said was important and I did not know why, for I was a child and he was a man. I did not understand the design then, so we did not speak of it directly. But when the Mother and I left the next day, he said to me, "One day you will know who I am, Mary, and when you do, know also that I wait to speak with you. I am your friend, and I will always be your friend. You may come to me at any time, and I will help you. When you remember who you are and why you are here, come to me and we will speak words together once more."

I had gone to see him again with the Mother Mary, after our return from the Sea of Galilee, at the beginning of my thirteenth year. He had been awaiting us, standing at his garden gate. He welcomed us and his woman, Naomi, gave us sweet figs and cakes, and we all sat together in the shade of the garden, speaking about the design.

I was very proud, then, for I had been initiated and had learned of the fields of force and knew that what we all were doing was very important. And he was so kind to me, listening to me and according me. I learned to put my pride away and to listen, and I learned of his intention to help Christ, and of his vital role in the plan.

His place in my heart was assured, for as I left, he detained me at the garden gate, saying,

"Mary, you are a great woman. You will learn humbleness and live the days of your life with courage, feeling the joy and the pain equally, holding not back, and for this I admire you. Know always that for you, I am here. Our souls have made the pact of union between, and I will honor it always above all else. One day, many years from now, the world will know what you have done, and will accord your greatness. They will acknowledge your place in the design. For now, know that I know who you are and that I admire you above all others. Because of the importance of what you have come to do, I have asked Naomi, my most trusted friend and companion, to attend you when you are ready to leave your family home and begin your healing work. She knows of the design and your calling and has chosen to assist you and support you in your unfoldment. She will love you and cherish you as I cannot, and be to you a symbol of my love and devotion."

He held out his arms and I went into them. We spoke no more words, feeling the union of our souls, crying with joy that we were together.
It would take many years for the resolution of the design, and we cried also from the sadness, and the joy and sadness wove a pattern between us, softened by our tears.

And now, so many years later, I felt the same joy and sadness merging within me. For this was the way of the human, the bright and the dark as one, seeking to be not judged.

And with the weaving came peace and strength and the commitment to live this life fully.

I arose, the shadows now gone from my garden and from my heart, the brightness and the darkness joined as one.

THE COURAGE OF MIRIAMNE

It was our last summer in Israel, and one day Christ and I arose early and set off for a long walk in the hills. The aridness of the land called us and we strode purposefully through the valleys and caverns, cherishing the richness of our days here, spending every possible moment together. As the sun heated the sky, bringing a blanket of fire to the Earth, we returned to my garden and lay together under the olive trees, savoring the shade and the stillness.

The time of the resurrection was close at hand, and Christ began speaking of his life and his passage and of those he would leave behind. He was tender and vulnerable, his words making pictures in the air between us. He spoke of his desire for union, the ideal of faith he had come to uphold, and his learning of the lesson of trust.

He reflected upon his childhood, speaking of his great love for his mother, of the passing of his father, and of his time of growing with his brothers and sisters. Lastly, he spoke of Miriamne, his cousin whom he called sister. She had helped his mother care for him when he was young.

He fondly remembered their early years, rolling in the dusty earth outside their home, teasing her with insects and spiders, and relived the bond of tenderness they had known.

She was soft and beautiful and proud, this sister of the Christ, and I admired her greatly. In the years since his return from the mountains they had grown apart, and he missed her presence in his life.

Her quality of nurturing gently brought one to comfort and solace, and as Christ spoke, I realized that it was this quality that had caused a separation between them.

Loving him as she did, she knew that to which he was being called. She had seen pieces of the design, seen Christ suffer and appear to die, and she was frightened for him, seeking to protect him. In the years when he and I were preparing for the crucifixion and resurrection Christ knew that she could not protect him, and so he had stayed apart from her. They both had mourned the loss of the other.

They loved each other dearly, and she was important to him. Her consciousness and awareness were pure, and he honored this, aware that in some way she was necessary for the fulfillment of the design. He felt the pain of their separation and desired to reach out to her, knowing that she was a part of the plan.

I felt that she should be told what we knew of the events which were to happen, or she would live her life feeling excluded, believing that he had died and that she had been unable to help him.

"Better for her to know than not to know," I said.
"If you do not tell her, then you are protecting her. Would it not be wise to see how she can participate?"

He pondered this for a moment and then agreed with me, and we ran the pathways to see what the outcome held, asking to be shown the best way for her to serve the design.

The resurrection was approaching, and Elisabeth and I were preparing to hold Christ's consciousness in transition between levels. We each needed another woman to help us: to be our eyes and our physical contact with the events as they unfolded. Elisabeth and I would need to believe in the reality of his life and not in the actions which would appear to result in his death. Judith would help Elisabeth, and the pathway showed to us that Miriamne would help me at that time. She would know that he was not killed, would understand the design fully, and know that she had been instrumental in helping him.

We knew now, that we should speak with her as soon as possible, to include her in the final preparations. I wanted to be the one to speak to her since our bond was crucial to the outcome, and so I climbed the hill to her home the next afternoon.

Wonderful smells of newly baked breads and cakes drifted from her door, and as I approached, I saw the children, three in number, playing in the trees beyond the house. They saw me approach, and as I came to the door, they ran to the house to see why I had come.

Miriamne appeared in the door frame before I could knock. She was clear as a brook of rapidly flowing water, with no pretense, and her emotions played freely upon her face. She was surprised and curious, awe struck and afraid. Her questions rose to the surface, and I quickly put up my hand.

"He is well," I said.

I watched relief gather to smooth the surface of the water, and then the questions boiled again to the top, and so I answered the most evident one.

"I have come to ask you to help us," I said.

She inclined her head and moved aside, and I entered the room. Lined on the tables before me were the baked goods which she was preparing for market. She took a fresh loaf of warm bread from the hearth and put it between us, indicating a chair for me and moving to prepare for us some brew. The children peeked at me through the door frame now, and Miriamne firmly told them to return to their games beneath the trees.

She came to sit across from me at the table by the hearth, and then asked, "What is it that I can do for you or for him, Mary Magdalena?"

Settling myself in the chair, I looked at her, telling her of how it had been for us so she would understand that to which she was being called.

"As you know, I have been helping Christ to bring the ways of knowledge to the world. I know that you have watched me and that we have been apart because we have never created between us an understanding. I have come here today, for I choose to create that understanding with you now, Miriamne. It is important to me and to Christ that this understanding be forged immediately. We are both loving you very much and now know that you are essential to the fulfillment of the design. I know that you have always seen him being condemned and appearing to die, but you have not seen the truth fully.

"There is nothing to fear. Your brother will be eternally at peace, and there is no reason for you to worry. Christ will not die, Miriamne. I can promise you that. For it is Elisabeth and I and Judith of the village, and you, if you agree, who will assure this. I have been training for many years to assist your brother in creating the illusion of his death on the cross and the reality of the resurrection. If you will sit with me now, I will show you those parts of the design which have been held from your awareness until this moment."

She inclined her head to me, tears standing unshed in her eyes. She was gentle and soft, as I have said, and so it took great courage to look at the records and to accord them and allow herself to absorb them completely. This, of course, was why she had not seen or known the truth of what was to come before.

I bade her close her eyes, and we held hands and ran the pathway between us, and she saw the design and her part in it.

I showed her the part that Christ and I called her to effect. She was afraid at first, looking at the design and then at the human events which would happen, and again at the design and back again at the events. And then she saw the distinction and surrendered to the knowing, realizing that she had been afraid, all of her life, because she had not had the courage to see the design and to follow it through to the end.

She had drawn human conclusions about the events and used the information to fuel the fear instead of resolving it.

I saw her change before me, becoming bolder and more assured.
I spoke to her, saying, "We must work together for many days now to see the pathways more clearly and to know each other more fully. We must learn to communicate without words and to trust in the design completely. You are being called because of your deep love of the Gods and of Christ and the purity of your soul. Christ and I came to see this last night, and so we invite you to be with us. He loves you very much and desires your presence and assistance as he is held between the levels."

She began to cry then, the tears streaming down her cheeks. She paid no attention to them however, according only the words I had spoken and the honor that she felt for Christ.

She did not withdraw her hands to wipe the tears from her cheeks, but sat with her hands in mine, no longer uneasy with me.

Then she spoke of it. "I have not been comfortable with you, Mary, for since he came to manhood, he has loved you as he has loved no other. I have watched you together, and there is a sensuality, and you have this also with Judas and with Thomas and with others. They come to you, and as you know, they do not come to me. I have not judged this as much as I have wondered of it. I have asked myself what it is about and why I am not a part of it, for I love him so much! And I have always felt a deep bond for him. Since I can first remember, I have cared for him as an older sister.

And then some years ago, I decided that I could do nothing to help him, and so I married and had my three children and have made my own life, apart from his.

"But, as you know, it has always lain heavy on my heart, for he is my favorite of all. And now that I have despaired of being of help to him and of resolving it, here you are. I cry because of the gift that I have received."

I knew by the tone of her voice and the carriage of her body that her choice to meet her greatest challenge had assured her place in the design. Her act of courage had resolved her fear, and she now was free to live the fulfillment of her calling.

Taking her hands from mine, she broke the bread before us, and offered me a piece. And as I ate of the loaf she asked me of my life and of my calling, and I told her of who I was. As we talked, I felt her weaving the fabric of peace between us, and I gave thanks.

Later that evening, after we had supped, I helped her pack her things and attend to her family, and then we went together down the hill, walking to the Mount of Olives where Christ awaited us.

THE TIME HAS COME

"I am afraid," said Judas.

"I know," said Christ. "I am afraid, also."

They stood together in the darkness outside my home, the final moments beginning. Judas had come to say good-bye, for it was time for him to go.

They stood very close, Christ and Judas, intent on their mission and on each other. They leaned together, their hands on each other's shoulders, looking purposefully into each other's eyes.

There was no deception. Each was equally committed to the moment, to the other, and to the design.

Even then the energy which the illusion would create was forming walls of separation which would become mistrust and hatred in the weeks and months to follow—walls of separation that would exist for 2000 years and be the core of the people's search for unity.

But now there was no separation, and Judas remained in this moment to assure the Christ and himself of this truth. He remained to affirm his love and loyalty to the one he had come to help, the one he loved as much as himself.

He knew it was time but held back the moment to savor the bond and affix the symbol of his love to the heart of the other.

Christ stood receiving this love, and they spoke again of the fear and the plan and the passing.

I listened because I loved them both and because there was nowhere else for me to go. The plan had cast us into this time of separation from the others.

I sensed their love for each other as waves of light and sound radiating from their bodies. Their pain was as real as their love, born from their concern for the safety of the other. They mourned the coming separation, and each in his own way questioned the outcome of what they had come to create—the illusion of betrayal.

They were alive, one for the other, in the way of men—in the way of soldiers, fathers, and sons, through the friendship that is joined in the loins.

They told of their love and embraced. Judas placed his right hand for one brief moment on Christ's heart and placed his left hand on his own heart. They stood thus, and the current of a bond which cannot be broken, even by time, passed between them.

Then Christ placed his right hand on the heart of Judas and his left hand over his own. As Judas received this tribute, I saw it fill the places of doubt and despair within him.

They spoke of their love one last time, each pledging his loyalty to the other. They trusted, but they were also uncertain.

290

The records were clear, but always there was free will. The people had free will, each free to choose action, belief, and reality. We felt a moment of fear. Would the design be accomplished as we had planned? Would Christ survive the cross and the state of transition between life and death? Would Judas survive the wrath of the others? Would we leave unscathed for France after the resurrection?

They broke apart. I felt a tearing deep within me, for I knew it would never be the same again. The leaving wrenched them also, and they stood for another moment, feeling safer together than apart.

As he turned to leave, Judas looked at me and nodded. In his eyes was the torment that had been there of late, the knowledge of what he must do and how it would appear to the people.

I blanched within, keeping my face in the frame of love and trust, not letting him see my fear. But he felt what was within me and reached out his hand. I took it, feeling his strength and his love flowing into me from his palm.

Then he was gone.
I sobbed, feeling angry for the way of it all.

I turned from my door and ran to the hills for help and solace.

Later, when I was more at peace, I looked back toward the city where the crucifixion would create upheaval for thousands of years, to the place where it would all begin—the people's greed and jealousy creating war, hatred, and oppression.

I sent a blessing to the people and the land, asking for the courage to live the design, and then I walked home.

I saw Christ then, standing by my garden gate where I had left him, his head now raised skyward, his arms open in a gesture which implored the heavens.

I joined him in my mind, sending him my love. I felt his questions, his hesitation, and his loyalty to the design. He truly remembered, and yet he felt torn within. We saw the conflict our actions were designed to create and the way the people would change the story and cease to trust, forgetting the truth and seeking earthly survival instead of the truth of the soul.

And in this moment we were all that was left, he and I. It seemed a telling of what would come more than sixty years in the future, the time when Christ and I would again be alone, facing the end together.

We moved at the same moment toward the other; and when he reached me, he held out his arms and I went into them. We stood crying silently, calling the ones without names to help us, for there was nowhere else to turn.

The night closed around us. Peace and assurance settled over us, and we played it one to the other. We sent out the flame to Judas, enveloping him in this peace and love and truth.

We felt him join us, and our love flowed between. And we pledged, we three, that through all time we would stay as one in the way of the heart.

THEY CAME FOR HIM
IN THE NIGHT

The Romans came for him in the night.
I remember it as a cool, crisp evening,
full of remorse and sharpness,
like a blade which cuts the edge from the dark.

I had wrapped a shawl around me,
and we stood quietly together Christ and I,
knowing the end
and the beginning
had come.

The time for the fulfillment of the design had come,
and we were afraid,
needing the support
and presence of the other
to continue.

We were unable to speak,
for there were no more words;
we had said them all.
And so we clung together
in my garden of Gethsemane,
preparing to part
and be physically separate
and more profoundly alone
than either of us had ever been before.

We knew the separation would pass
and that we would find each other again,
but it would not be
until after the crucifixion,
and there was still so much which was uncertain.

So many people were a part of the plan,
and of course, each had free will.
What if something went wrong
and we were never able to be together
again in the same way: body to body,
heart to heart, life to life?

Steadfastness flowed between us,
forged from the difficult trials
we had faced together.
Now suddenly,
there was to be one event,
one moment in time
that would affect
the course of mankind
for thousands of years to come.

We were the players, all of us,
dedicated to the outcome.
Yes, it would be fine after all.
The perfection of the design assured it.
And yet, and yet—
so much depended on each of us.

We held each other more tightly as these thoughts
coursed through our minds,
and the current ran between our hearts.

We knew it would only be three days;
that he, as Christ,
would transcend the veil of the body
and fly home,
and then return, committed
to the fulfilling of his prophecy.

And I would stay behind,
preparing the way for his return,
keeping the levels open
to let him go
and receive him again.

And in the garden that last night
Christ and I stayed
heart to heart,
pouring our love back and forth,
merging our integrity and our strength.

I prepared him as best I could,
giving him my love and my light
and my assurance.

He pledged to me
the undying connection of light
through the spectrum of time.
He did this with his being,
and I received it as a gift,
long awaited.

We whispered softly,
for the others were at the garden gate
awaiting his return.

297

We spoke of the remaining days,
affirming the plan,
reciting our roles.

One last time he looked into my eyes,
taking his big, broad hands
and cupping my small face within them.
We reached beyond the garden
into the creation and the force of life
which abounded there.
Calling forth the records,
we flew on the pathway of information
there encoded.

We saw unity
forged through the choice
of our consciousness
to experience it.

And the flames within us
merged again
rising ever higher,
carrying us even more
into the other,
forging us as one.

Quickly he withdrew,
knowing it was time.
Tension gathered around us,
splitting the molecules of air.

I felt as if I lost the connection
for a moment,
but as he moved away
we stayed joined, balanced
without the other's physical presence.

When I felt centered again,
I nodded.
His eyes told me all
that he could not say.

And he was gone.

When they came for him,
I heard the commotion,
felt the tensing of his body
and his conscious control
of his breath and his thinking.

I knew when they had gone, for
the tension lessened and there was silence;
there was again peace in my garden,
the birds coming to
form a circle around me.

I stayed there for a long time
having nowhere to go,
feeling that as long as I was not with him
there was never anywhere else to go.

I linked my mind to his
and stayed with him,
sending him my presence through our bond.
I prayed, too,
that all would proceed
according to the highest good
of all concerned,
for so much depended on spirit
and our ability to stay attuned with it.

I knew when they had placed him in the cell, for
I felt him become quiet, breathing more regularly.
The dew of the night then
awakened me to the fact
that I was cold
and stiff
and alone.

I shivered, walking slowly to my home,
to the remains of the meal
we had shared that morning.
I threw the food to the birds
and put the dishes away,
gathering my courage
to face my first night alone,
knowing there would be many more.

We had shared many moments of aloneness
in the last months
preparing for tonight
and for what was yet to come.
Now all would change,
and we must ready ourselves to leave this place.

Although I was ready to go,
the physical act distressed me.
The actual leaving made the design more real
and more unreal at the same time.

I knew I did not belong here,
yet, while I longed to be gone,
this land was all
that I had ever known.

It was difficult, for I could not tell anyone good-bye.
My family and friends did not know I would leave,
and I would be gone before they knew why.

My solace came from knowing that
some of those I truly loved
would go with me,
but some would not,
and I knew I would never see them again
in this physical life.
And so I mourned—
not only for the human loss
in the way of the world's grieving,
but because there were so many
who would not remember
and be left with the cross of unknowing.

I sighed
and brought to me my animals,
turned down the lamp, and
faced the darkness.

In the morning I would face them all,
and it would take courage,
almost as much courage as it had taken
to say good-bye
to Christ tonight:
my truest light.

I prayed for his safety
and peace
and that he remember,
for in the remembering
is the freedom
from the fear.

I felt his head on my breast in that moment,
and then we slept,
he in the Romans' prison,
and I
on the mount
with the olives.

And we walked in our dreams,
he to me and I to him,
meeting in the place of all lovers,
in the heart
that has no form
and   remembers   all.

THE RECKONING OF
PONTIUS PILATE

He stood facing me, his robes flowing in thick folds away from his body. Majesty radiated from his being, and yet I sensed that this was cultivated—an illusion he created and set into motion around him.

He tested me immediately, sending his dogs to me from their position by his altar-like throne. There were six of them, large and powerful, bred for fierceness. He kept them with him often, their presence helping him to wield his power and strength. I knew that he had ordered them toward me to disquiet me, and that they would not hurt me—he hoped to take the edge of the blade of power from me.

I stood my ground, which is the path of power with all creatures, and began a soft humming sound in my throat. The sound was inaudible to Pilate and yet sensed immediately by his hounds.

They stopped in their path, heads to the side, listening now for the message of the sound. I went deep into the memory of their origin, into the fiber of being, singing them the lullaby of their instinct, which is much deeper than any man's training. I gave them the command to lie down in their place and they did so without hesitation.

As his dogs lay down, Pilate became angry, ordering them harshly to return to their kennels. His man, who had been standing away from us at a distance, did not look at me. I had bested Pilate, and he could not acknowledge it. He silently took them, closing the door softly behind him.

I could see Pilate's thoughts wrapping around his form, sustaining the illusion of power and strength which he sought to portray. I felt a weakness within him, a weakness of disposition, a lack of personal decisiveness, and a longing for acceptance which would not be granted him because he did not inspire it. His lack of integrity was felt by the people around him, but was belied by their seeming deference to him.

All pretense aside now, we stood facing each other.

"You know why I have come, Pilate?" I asked.

"Yes of course, you have come to beg for the life of the man that you love. What is his name now, oh yes, the man called Christ."

"Pilate, let us put aside our differences so that our conversation may yield us the desired results," I said.

"Your desired results, you mean," he snickered.

"Pilate, there is one design and one outcome, and we both know what that outcome will be and how it will appear. You and I are servants of the people and must guide them into knowledge and truth as best we can.

The time has come for the reckoning: the reckoning of you, me, Christ, the disciples, and the people. Our choices are important to the outcome. Your choice is important to the outcome. Will you at least accord this?" I asked him.

"Do you not understand?" he replied. "I do not care about the design. It has brought me nothing. I have made my own way. I care only for the body and the power, for this is all that will withstand the test of the people. They have long ago forgotten the truth and the way. Yes, I know of what you speak, and it is no longer real for me, for I have seen what works here, and it is not love and peace and the choice for justice."

He became incensed, screaming at me, "It is power that assures one's place, and I will triumph! You will see. I have power, and he does not. Of course, long after we have gone he will have power, but now, now is when the power is to be wrested from the people! Now! For now is all that matters. You will see!"

I told him then of the time to come, and he listened, darkly perceiving the events which were to follow. I saw him and did not see him at the same time. We faced each other through the mists of vision, and he cloaked himself from me, but I knew him nevertheless.

Absentmindedly, he fingered the richly thick garment that he wore. His fingers, adorned with rings of precious jewels, shone brightly in sharp contrast to the darkness within him.

His power had corrupted his spirit, overlaying it with the tarnish of money and greed for material things. He loved the women and the men equally, going from one bed to the other, seeking only pleasure, for he had no real pleasure otherwise, no happiness from within.

I told him again why I was there and of the actions he could take to assure the fulfillment of the design. I knew that he was aware of what was to happen, that he knew who I was in the overall plan and was conscious of his choices and the outcomes he would create by those choices.

I knew before I came what his response would be and how he would react to me, but the ones with no names had told me to come, and so I did.

He was a pretender, a disguiser; one who had called the forces around him to create illusion, and his time had come, the time of his reckoning.

I was a part of that reckoning, here to give him the chance to change his mind, to help in the design, and to accord his spirit.

I was not surprised when, at the end of our speaking, he raised his hand toward me and ordered the power to come through his arm, sending me away with venom on his tongue and acid in his heart. He turned his mind away from his spirit and purpose, hating me, for I reminded him of both.

"I wash my hands of you and of him and your alleged purpose here in my city," he spat at me. "I disdain you and your followers and the poor people who so desperately seek your truth! Go from here and do not return, for the Romans have no room in their hearts for you, or the followers, or the One."

And I knew he had betrayed himself when he spoke of Christ as "the One," for it meant that he truly knew who he was.

But I kept my thoughts neutral: I did not judge him and did not think of
the plan or the Roman then, for Pilate was wary and sharp and greedy,
and his insecurity made him suspicious of everyone.

I spoke clearly and distinctly to him, the man who would condemn Christ.

"It will be as you wish it, Pilate," I said, "for it is your decision, is it not?
And it is your pathway of power that will be decided also."

And I walked away from him steadily, turning not my back to him.
When I reached the door I opened it, and bowing to him, was gone.

THE CRUCIFIXION OF
JESUS CHRIST

I took up my position on the side of the mountain, praying quietly with my eyes closed. I awaited Miriamne, who was to be with me when Christ was brought to Golgotha.

My body trembled, and my hands moved uncontrollably beneath my cloth. I clasped them together to stop their movement. I felt my body contracting in waves of terror. I continued to breathe deeply, forcing the fear away with my knowing, over and over again, until it diminished, and the knowing was stronger than the fear.

I loved him so much and longed to be with him so that he could see my eyes upon him, but I knew that what I did was necessary and would, in the end, be of more help to him than my being there with him.

I could hear the people below me, their voices raised, and I could feel the tension mounting, their hatred asserting itself in the violence that turned them away from their very souls.
They crucified themselves, not him.
They denied their own divinity, not his.
They sought to crush their own hatred and desperation
by hating him and living in separateness from him.

Waves of terror mounted again within me, and I shuddered. I knew he would feel my body as I was feeling his, so I again breathed and brought my knowledge through me to calm myself.

I could feel Elisabeth waiting for Judith as I waited for Miriamne, and I sent her the energy of my conviction that we would affect the outcome we had accorded together.

The faces of the people rose before me, and I knew they were the faces Christ saw also. Their hatred brought me to my knees, and I cried from the depths of my soul for justice and for the loving to return to their hearts, and I vomited the bile of the race of humanity that it would turn such against itself.

Then I felt hands gently lifting me upright, and I looked up into the eyes of Miriamne. There was strength there in her face that I needed, and love there that I needed, and faith there that lit her face and my heart, and she embraced me, and we cried out that the world was such.

Her strength seeped into me, and her light brought me to the light of my knowing again, her faith showing me that the design we prayed for would be created.

"It is time, Mary," she said.

I pulled myself back, as if from a long distance, and felt her presence and the presence of Elisabeth and Judith, and we began.

I closed my eyes and faced Elisabeth on the other side of Golgotha. Miriamne and Judith looked below us at the crowd that was forming as Christ made his way up the hillside with the cross.

They stood behind us, their hands resting upon our shoulders, speaking continually of the events which were happening below.

Elisabeth and I attuned first one to the other, balancing the waves of energy between us and creating a field of resonance in which Christ could place his being. As we breathed, I felt her breath match mine, and I gave thanks.

We stretched our union taut, keeping the pathway clear. Miriamne and Judith spoke to us of what they saw, and Elisabeth and I maintained a field of light between us, holding Christ's being in union with God and the fiber of being within the field.

Then I felt this field of light become the presence of God as I had not known before here on Earth. Christ felt this presence at the same moment, and we surrendered, guiding the fields, yes, but knowing also that it was now assured, for all the realms were assisting us.

Christ was caught and held in the ray of creation and, as we breathed, he fused again with light, and his body was not the place wherein his consciousness lay.

He ceased to feel pain or strife or struggle, resting in the arms of his Father and Mother.

And the Earth

O P E N E D

and began to pour

Her energy upon humankind

showering them with the

RAIN OF TRANSFORMATION.

The trees burst forth with a loud

thundering of force

and all was

split   a s u n d e r

and the new energy of

c r e a t i o n

flowed forward into

the light of being.

316

And the wind
and the rain

and the lightning
and the thunder

were the voices of the Earth
which were raised
for the unlistening—
and they heard.

The hatred and vengeance of mankind
were reflected
back to them,
and they were sore afraid.

All was a mirror
for the strife
that was created
moment by moment
in this life.

There was no escape.
The mirror was clearly
and more clearly
a reflection
of the disorder
and chaos
of the people.

They realized the unleashing of the storm
as a sign of their need
to choose more wisely,
to create more completely,
and allow more fully.

The old was dying,
and they were a part of the new
because they had survived.

A part of them was
relieved that the old
was dead
and that they were free
to be a part of the new order.

The storm was a symbol of sacrifice,
transmutation,
and integration.
And they were well pleased.

The order of the world was reformed,
and there was a new place
to behold the light
and abide in the truth.

The storm was a signal of a release
from old beliefs and structures,

a signal of the ability
to design the plan anew
without boundary or limitation,
totally from the flow
of the juices of knowing
from within.

Although there was no clear pattern,
the people were aware of the readiness of their spirit
to undertake this new creation.
And they were well contented.

Christ had told them of the seed of light within them,
that aspect of the soul which had now been awakened.
It gave to them the vision for the creation of their destiny
here in the world.

They had listened with their hearts,
and their souls were awakened
to the light within.
They were merged with the light
as they listened,
which brought them into peace.

He had spoken of the need for unity
and affirmed their journeys as a symbol
of a search for something
already within them.

He had given them the words
about love,

telling them of God's kingdom,

and giving them keys to this kingdom

as surely as if he had

d   d

r   e

o   p

p

a

g e m

into their awareness.

THE LEAVING

I stood before the mantel as the sun set behind me casting shadows of golden-orange light upon my shoulders. I had only a few hours to pack and prepare to leave the place called Jeru-salem. I could take with me only a small sack of belongings, leaving behind almost all of what I had come to own.

A shiver ran involuntarily through my body. There were arrangements to make, and I must see the Roman yet again. But I tarried here, feeling for the last time the presence of my home and my belongings.

Christ was with Joseph of Arimathea, our friend, our truest friend, who had kept Christ safe while he was in transition. Joseph and I sat by the tomb together, holding the forces between the worlds so that Christ could come and go without harm.

There was a void created through the time dimension, and it could close upon him at any moment unless we held it open in the position necessary to assure his passage between worlds and back into this one.

So we had waited, Joseph and I, and kept the vigil; when others would come to pay their respects or to pray at the grave site or to seek in curiosity the slain Christ, he would hold them away from me, leaving me undisturbed.

I appeared to mourn deeply and pray constantly to the Lord of my keeping when, in fact, I knew he was not gone but only away. I was within the frame of the structure, holding and balancing all of the worlds simultaneously, with help from the lights and the beings. Elisabeth, Miriamne, Judith, Naomi, the Mother Mary, and my earthly mother helped also, and we were working on all sides of the void together.

I would force the tenseness from my shoulders through my intention and remain there, by his body, in the constancy necessary to affect the result.

I had seen him only briefly before he had been placed in the tomb, with many in attendance and with no words spoken, of course, for he was presumed dead. We were even then maintaining him in the state which appeared to others as the mask of death.

We kept him in accordance with the rhythms as the force of life diminished and was replaced with the cadence of the template of the order of being.

He ceased to exist as a mortal soul and was carried on the wave of creation into the void. We held the soul in transition until the body returned to normal consciousness and could again contain the soul which had been within.

There were many levels to be opened and maintained, and I did this for him now as I would at the time of his true mortal death, over 60 years in the future.

For now, we had created the illusion of his "death" to assure the design of the resurrection, so that the people would know that the soul is immortal. There would then come a time when the people would remember that within their immortal soul is the knowing that they are spirit in form. Then there would be no separation between them and God, between them and spirit, or between them and each other. They would understand the unity of all souls and the revolving of the circle of creation: spirit into form into spirit.

Christ was now within that circle, in the realms of transition. He awaited me, somewhat weakened and perplexed. His memory was not fully re-established, and he drifted in and out of consciousness, between dimensions. It would be Joseph and I and the others who would stand guard for him so that he could physically leave Jeru-salem unmolested.

Thomas and Judas and Christ and I would go, and there were others who would follow later, and those who would not. There would be those who would stay and teach and die, and those who would challenge the souls of the unbelieving through words and example and prophecy.

As I stood in my house remembering, I knew I must act, knew it was time, and yet I tarried here, my eyes moving to the objects I would take and embracing the ones I would leave.

I was reluctant to go because I knew that the design was not yet over, would not be over for longer than 60 years, and there were still many days to live and many lessons to be learned and much aloneness ahead of me.

I knew I must act, and yet when I did, I would begin the end. I would begin the next phase of my pattern, my next turning.

I brought my attention back to the room. I must leave no sign of where I had gone or how I would go. I must think as they would think in their determination to find us, because I would be most suspect; the Romans who would follow me knew that I was the closest one to Christ.

I shivered again, as if someone were walking on my grave. And perhaps they were, for many would think that I had died, that Judas had died, that we had all been killed in the night by the Romans, or that we had taken our own lives, or fled into the hills. They would not think, at least in the beginning, that we had gone by boat.

The Roman soldier would make sure that we were not followed, at least until we were cleanly away. I must attend now to the final details of the arrangements with him. It would be our last time together, and this saddened me. I would then visit Christ and Joseph, returning to pack my few belongings. I would sleep until the deep silence of the night called me, stealing away then into the night's darkness, leaving the Mount of Olives that I loved.

I felt pain at the thought of leaving, although, as I have said, I never did belong here.

I squared my shoulders and left the room and my house, and walked swiftly down the hill.

PEACE ON MY MOUNTAIN
PEACE IN MY GARDEN

I dreamt that I was awakened by gunshots.
There were gunshots on the Mount of Olives.

The people were fighting, nation to nation,
and there was no peace in the city of Jeru-salem
or in the sacred land of Israel.

And in my dream I arose from my bed and ran into the night.

As I stepped onto the land, the mother Earth trembled,
and the sound of her tears was one with the sound
of the guns' fire.

As I looked into the night,
it was not my world, not my time.

It was the time of the remembering—
the time when the people would turn from their fear and
judgement and remember their unity.

But first the guns would fire,
and the people would die and fly home,
and the world would know killing and war,
hatred and violence.

And in my dream I walked to the edge of the mountain,
seeing all that would be, knowing all that would
come to pass.

And the wrath and the vengeance of the world came around me,
and I shuddered,
speaking these words to the hearts of the people:

"It has been many years
since there was peace on my mountain.

The design has afforded the people
the opportunity to choose their destiny
as it relates to themselves and others,
and therefore to history.

As I look at the choices,
I shudder to think that
we have created such an outcome.

We had known it would take many years to be seen—
the truth—
but what was created
in the meantime is difficult to behold.

"And yes, my garden was as any other garden,
except that this place was a

c h a m b e r

o f   s i l e n c e

a n d   s o u n d

which bade the levels to create in form
and to carry and store the knowledge within the trees,
and within the land,
and within the sacred spaces of being.

There will again be peace in my garden, rest assured.

For all of the plans and the revelations are coming
within now

and then, of course, without.

Protect   my   garden,

for   herein   lies   the

secret to the harmony which you seek

to create in the world.

"We are with you all, and I am with you:
and we are women together, first;
and sisters together, second

and souls together, third;
and forces of love together, fourth;
and change-agents of the world together, fifth;
and sixth—we are the   Goddesses   of all time,

come to

r e c l a i m

o u r

p o w e r

t h r o u g h

t h e   e m e r g e n c e

o f   t h e   t r u t h

o f   a l l   t i m e.

We are now ready
to be suspended within the minds of men,

and our duty lies
in the observance of the truest design of mankind
which has ever been lived.

"AND IT IS WRITTEN:

There will be among all the people
the peace of a million years of dreaming.
And it will come to pass
that there will be no separation.

The people will rise together,
young and old,
female and male,
and there will be equality.

And all nations shall be as stars
shining from the same sky
with the same intention:
to light the way for mankind.

The days shall number years
and millenniums,
and it will come to pass
that these moments
are all the same,
simultaneous.

Then all the knowledge
and all the words of learning
will be reborn
into the awareness,
and all will be understood.

The questions
will be answered,
the meanings known.

"And there will be
no more aloneness,
for the people
will reach out
from their souls
and their hearts.
And their visions
will be of unity,
truth, and order.

The ways of mankind
will become the ways
of the angels,
and there will be
the coming together of all ages
in one moment.

And the learnings
will at last
be clear.

The people
shall rejoice
and dance within,
and all the kingdoms
shall rise together,
as if from the mist
of the dreams
of humanity,
and forge a union
with the divine.

"The way
shall be lighted
with the truth
from the spheres.

And man shall join woman
in the final dance
of alchemy.

All despair
shall be lifted
and transformed
into the rainbow
of peace.

There shall be no war,
no famine,
and no pestilence.
For the Lord
and the Goddess
shall merge—
and the night
and the day.

All of the forces
shall come together
to signal
the end
and the beginning.

"The belief of duality
will be laid to rest,
and all dichotomy
shall pass away.

The people
will remember
and search no more.

Their feet and their hands,
their hearts
and their souls,
shall merge
within and without.

The microcosm
shall become
the macrocosm.

The moments
shall merge
to be experienced
as time
standing still.

Each moment
shall embrace
all desire and all need,
fulfilling
their greatest
longings.

"There will be no
loss or abandonment,
for all will be made known.

The Father and the Mother
shall join hands across the sky,
embracing all their children
in the crystal light of being.

And they will rest forever,
the children,
in the bosoms of truth and love,
and all else will pass away.
And so it is written."

And   so   it   is.

Peace in our garden.

ON OUR WAY

In the middle of the night on the third day, Joseph of Arimathea sent to me a messenger, for it was time to leave Israel.
He had hidden Christ within a cart filled with wares and vessels designated for the trade and had fulfilled the plans for our escape.

I had said a painful good-bye to the Roman, and the aching tenderness of his embrace enfolded me still, our last holding. I was now joining the others to begin the long journey to the sea.
Thomas, Judas, Christ and I were going together. Later, the Mother Mary, Naomi, Elisabeth, and Peter would follow us. Matthew and John would go into the hills, and later many would travel to the Grecian Islands, to the places where knowledge would be recorded.

I quickened my pace as the messenger directed me to the meeting place. I saw Joseph ahead; the darkness and the secrecy mixed, blended into a darkness I felt within my very soul.

Joseph held out his arms, and I went into them. This was also our last holding. I loved him as a father, for that is what he had been to me. His look assured me that everything was in order for the voyage. It would be many moons before we came to rest in a place where we could live and love freely—a place near the mountains of France. The voyage would be long and arduous, and we all felt within us the mixture of grief and a longing for the freedom to breathe the air of our own convictions.

Judas awaited me now, touching my shoulder as Joseph released me. He took my hand and led me into the night.

I remember the darkness and the parting and the knowing that we would all meet again in some way at some time, knowing that we would all be together again.

The players. In 2000 years, we would all be together again.

MY SECOND TURNING

UNTIL WE MEET AGAIN

"I must go," Christ said to me.
"I know."

"Do you know how long it will be before we are together again?"
"Yes."

"Will you be all right?"
"Yes."

"You seem so disturbed."
"I am."

"For God's sake, Mary, speak to me!"
"I cannot."

For the first time he was at a complete loss,
for I had withdrawn my energy from him,
and I had never done that
in all of the years of our knowing.

So Christ took me in his arms and held me,
caressing me as if I were a small child,
running his hands through my hair
in the way that I so loved.

I began sobbing, but only after long moments of stoic withdrawal,
attempting to disavow my pain and my fear. For both were with me in full
force, the years and the miles ahead without him full upon me.

I wanted the pain to stop, and the time to be over, the work to be done, and for us to be home.

In the six years since the crucifixion it had been harder, the apparent betrayal creating doubt and mistrust among the people. The energy had changed; the people did not believe in anything, yet they held to the hope that the legends and prophecies would come to pass.

There were many who tried to fulfill the prophecies, and they were laughed at or stoned or spat at with contempt. Some were even crucified.

Through my sobs I heard him say, "I love you too much to go. It is too much."

I waited to reply because I was overcome and because I wanted him to stay and I hoped, for a moment, that we could create it that way.

Then I sighed, saying, "No. We must do it because we have chosen this as our destiny.

"You must go to India to minister to the people there, and I must stay here in France with Judas and Naomi. I will bear my children and teach of our pathway so that the learnings will continue when we are gone. We must live our callings and be apart until it is time for us to be as one again, before our human passing."

"My Mary, my Mary. Will any other live this pain of separation such as we live? Will our living it stop them from living it? Do we change anything by what we do?"

But he did not really expect an answer because he knew the answer—knew that we must all go through the pain to remember that it is but an illusion, and the only way to find home is through the learning.

He held me again, and we lay under the dark sky with no stars or moon in attendance, nature affirming the darkness we felt.

We cried, holding each other as if for the last time. And oh, how many times had seemed to be the last.

We held each other closer and closer, trying to stave off the parting with our love, keeping in the place of our oneness, as if to protect us from what was to come.

At last we slept, and the angels came in our dreams and touched our brows and wiped away the pain, and plucked out the darkness with their wings.

When we awakened, we were at peace. Christ said good-bye to Judas and Naomi, and we made preparation for the parting, planning our reunion, many years in the future.

He started off as the sun rose over the mountain. I watched him until he was out of sight, and I stood alone, not moving, until Naomi came to fetch me hours later, holding me, lending me strength from her presence.

Finally, we turned in the midday sun, and I squared my shoulders, knowing I must live through it, but not knowing how. So I prayed again, oh again, for the courage to live the design.

My Firstborn

The birthing was complete, and Naomi lifted my firstborn son into the dim light of early morning. As the after-fluids rushed from my body, I felt a peace within me as my cells relaxed, remembering their old form.

As through a dream-glass, I watched Naomi gently place the child on my belly and heard her speak to him softly, waiting for his breath and sound before cutting the cord. She spoke to me softly, but with insistence.

"Mother, call him forth now, bring him in."

Where I was there was no form, and I drifted with him in that space between worlds. I must lead him into form, show him the way, for that is why he had come to me, but I felt hesitant, suddenly unsure of what I was to do. I had birthed so many, assisting my sisters as Naomi now assisted me. I understood the ambivalence I had witnessed in them, feeling the desire, as they had, to stay with him in spirit, to travel with him to all the dimensions—no form, no language, no rules, no world, no limitations. I would have to watch him grow and learn and succeed and fail, and I fought the temptation to keep him safe—unborn—held in the crystal clarity of transition.

At that same moment I breathed into him my light and my vision of his purpose and showed him the bridge.

He shuddered, catching the vision of light within him, and took his first breath, the sound catching in his throat and exploding the waters in his breathing tube.

353

His cough broke the stillness of the dawn. Then came his cry, born from the loins of his manhood. His body arched, and he breathed the substance of the Earth for the first time. He became human.

Naomi cut the cord which bound us, his life suddenly separated from mine. He was now vulnerable to the chill of this morning, to the need for food and shelter, love and security, to the aloneness of humanness.

This was the crucial moment, and Naomi's eyes sought mine as she placed him lovingly in my arms. I brought him to my breasts and wove the beating of my heart into the rhythm of his breath, bringing love all around him, speaking to him from my soul of our oneness with each other and with spirit. I played for him his passage from light into form and waited, waited for him to accord it.

As he did, his body relaxed against me, his mouth seeking my nipple, and he began to suckle.

I felt Naomi clean me and remove the birthing linens. My son and I lay together, sinking into the warmth of the new cloths she laid over us, and we slept.

I awoke with the feeling that something was wrong, that something was absent. I no longer held life within me. I remembered the birthing and opened my eyes to look at my body and my breasts, but there was no child. I looked up and saw Judas, my husband, standing over me, watching, waiting for me to awaken.

His luminescent eyes, full of light and fluid, shone with gratitude and awe. His hands, big and wide, cradled the child; yet his eyes did not leave my face. He held the child suspended between us as I breathed with relief to see our son. He watched me shyly, as if he had never seen my face before, his eyes filled with the magnitude that this moment held for him.

Intently, he said, "He is so small, my son!"
The first words were bold and boisterous, and the last, softer.
His voice challenged the stillness of the morning, but the child did not seem disturbed; rather, I felt their bond and was relieved.

Judas spoke again, "Magdalena, he is strong, our son."

I felt his vulnerability and saw doubt and worry cross his face. He was afraid I would reject him and he wanted me to forgive his absences and allow him to be a part of the bond I shared with the child. He asked that we join together in this special moment and that I accept him. I knew he was bonded to the child and that the space had been bridged, but he did not know I knew. . . or perhaps, yes, perhaps he did know and gave me the honor of affirming it.

"Yes, Judas, he is strong, our son!"

His eyes brimmed with tears as he bowed his head. I felt his hesitation, his clumsiness, his need to be distant from me dissolving in that moment as he stood before me. He sobbed, his eyes searching mine, saying, "I was so afraid, afraid he would be hurt or maimed or unfit because of what I have done." And he sobbed again, his breath catching in his chest.

The child watched Judas with no sign of fear, content to be held there in his hands. Judas felt the acceptance of his child and looked at me. Seeing that there was no holding-back, no judgement, his sobs turned to laughter, and he acknowledged his joy. Placing the child between us, he lay down beside me.

Tentatively, he reached out his hand to me and touched my face. "You are well, Magdalena?"

"Yes, Judas, I am well."

"You bear me no malice for staying away?"

"I bear you no malice."

Leaning on one arm he looked down at me, saying, "I seem to delight in bearing it all unto myself." He laughed ruefully.

"This one," he said, inclining his head to the child, "did you see how he has watched me, unafraid? Did you see how he cries not and attends my every word?" He waited for my acknowledgment, so I nodded in agreement.

"He is perfect, is he not, his body, his mind? And he is *my* son! Magdalena, perhaps it is as you have always said, that we are a blessed part of the design. Some of the time, when I think of the future, of who I am, of how I will be seen, how I *am* seen. . . " he paused, "I will remember this blessedness. This child, this gift, has brought to me this message."

356

As he looked at me there was no pretense or self-judgement or holding back. "Sometimes I am so alone, and I know you are alone also. I want to be with you, to be one with you, and yet something holds me away. Something I do not yet understand keeps me from loving you or myself, because the pain of the aloneness forces out the memory that there is love, that it is real for me, for us. I forget that you are one with me, and I live in the caves of darkness within my own soul, always searching for the way out. And I never find it. I feel only guilt for staying away from you; and so I come back, but I am not really here, and so I leave again."

He sighed. "This child. . . in some way this child will make a difference, has made a difference. I know this, and it gives me faith. Do you know what it is for me, Judas Iscariot, to have faith?"

His face reddened then and his eyes began to close him away from me, so I said, "Judas, stay here with me awhile. I have been alone also. The child brings our dreams into being yet again."

And in my eyes I opened my soul to him, and he stayed there with me.

He did not leave my bed for three days other than to feed the animals. Naomi attended us and would come to help me with the linens and freshen my body when he was gone.

He talked of his days to our son and to me, of his searching, of his pain, of his aloneness, and of his dreams. We listened, the child with his big grey-blue eyes and jet black hair, intent on each of his words.

I watched Judas change from a man with questions and uncertainty to a man assured and confident, full of the knowledge that it was his calling to teach his son.

We called him John, talking to him about all that we knew, counting his fingers and toes, touching his body, and singing to him the lullabies of our peoples.

On the third day as John lay sleeping, Judas took from me my robes and laid them aside. He stroked and kneaded my muscles and soothed my body, loving me tenderly, kissing me in all the places that I so loved. He brought the new assurance of his fatherhood into his love-making, the knowledge of his maleness coming forth to fill me. I felt renewed and safe. He gave to me from his life force in tribute for the life of our son which I had given him. And as he loved me in my body, he nurtured me in my soul, giving me a gift, the gift born of his gratitude.

For in the birth of his son, Judas had birthed himself.

THE TEARS OF NAOMI

I remember my last night in France—

       languid heat   pulsing clouds   sorrowful stars

The night I was lost in the web of illusion.
Naomi and I sat by the fire, the darkness lit by candles.

I watched her weave the layers of cloth through her sewing loop, gathering them into the folds which would adorn my shoulders. She bent deliberately over the task, matching the stitches, side to side. She did everything that concerned me with deliberation, for her loyalty and devotion had remained unchanged through all the years of her service.

The furs beneath her softened her sitting. They brought warmth to her old legs, and she smiled with contentment. I had bought the furs for her before we left Israel so that she would be warm and comfortable.

She sighed, and I saw her thoughts. She missed Israel—her family, the olive trees, the bustle of Jeru-salem, Joseph of Arimathea, her childhood home. We made new homes here, journeying many days in between, but she longed for one place, one home, all things familiar. . . as it was when we were first together. Oh to see again the home on the Mount of Olives— all the people coming, coming each day, the healing and the joy, the disciples, all of them, loving and sharing and talking and laughing. Now there were no people, just her and me and Judas and, now, Martha.

Since leaving Israel we had stayed apart from the people. Some from Israel still sought us, and we moved often for safety. We changed our dwelling place with each season, living at times with others in their homes or finding shelter in the Earth—in her mountains or caves or valleys. My children were now grown and gone, finding their own callings, and Naomi was lonely for the love and fulfillment of family and home.

She felt alone, but she had known this would be. When Joseph of Arimathea had first asked her to serve me, he had shown her the calling and the pathways. She was young and excited and proud to be asked, and so she had said yes even though she had seen the full design.

She had served me as a sister and a mother and a lover would, nurturing my body and my mind and my soul. When the people came to me for healing, Naomi prepared them, speaking to them of their fears and their longings, guiding them to calmness. Afterwards she soothed them, helping them to integrate their experiences.

She and the Mother Mary had met often in their intention to help me in the success of my calling, for its living was important for us all, and their guidance shaped its fulfillment.

When it was almost time to leave Israel, Naomi had seen her destiny again. This time I had shown her the pathways. She had seen the hiding and the moving, and the babies she would help me birth, and the family we would create together, the union we would share. She had seen the aloneness, my leaving Judas, going in search of the Christ.

And she had seen her final journey; her journey to Israel, old and alone, seeking again the peace and joy of her early days. But she knew her place was to be with me, and she had not hesitated to give her assent to the plan.

It was the first time that she knew her importance to the outcome— the first time her special place in my life was accorded, for there was no one else who knew the choices we were making, no one else I trusted as completely.

Naomi knew that no one could have taken care of me as devotedly as she had, and so she was content. I depended on her, so there was no real choice—it was only a knowing, and she followed it.

She finished her sewing and slowly folded the material, placing it on her lap, but she did not rise. It was almost time for us to move again, but this time was different. She sensed that we would not be together in the same way, that it was time for our parting.

I continued to follow her thoughts.

Since Martha had found us, we had lived in deception and denial. Chattering like a bird, Martha seemed carefree and light-hearted. She tried to join us as family, but Naomi saw the pretense in her actions. She did not trust her and tried to shield me from her deception.

I grew more quiet, reacting to Martha's presence, living more from my fear than my knowing.

Judas was distant and aloof, closed and silent. Acting more and more as a man wronged, he dared to be challenged. Slipping away even more frequently, he neglected his chores, returning only to sup with us.

Day after day, the tension mounted. Each meal we shared more difficult, more strained.

Naomi suspected that Martha slipped out to join Judas in the night. Several weeks after Martha's arrival, Naomi had awakened in the darkness and gone to relieve herself. Martha's bed cloths were empty, and Naomi did not hear her return. As the days passed Naomi watched my eyes grow darker and Martha's grow brighter, and she knew.

The tension built and added to the strain between me and Judas. Naomi tried to help us as she had done so many times in the past, bringing us to the realization of our love. But we listened not—each on our lonely path, not according the other. We lived separate lives.

This night, after we had supped, she took Judas and me aside and told us of her feelings, for she loved us both.

She said, "Your love is deeper than your distress. Why do you not remember this love?"

Our faces had closed as she spoke, and she saw that it was too late. She began to cry, pleading with us, saying, "It is time for the final parting, this I know, but you can part in love!"

She was frightened because she felt us close our hearts to her and to her words, and she began to sob. Judas, angry at Naomi's interference, retreated into the night. I stayed with Naomi.

Judas had gone to Martha, and we knew it. Naomi saw my face set in the resolve which marked my courage, my fear, and my aloneness.

Naomi breathed her knowing and said, "Mary, leave it alone! Leave it! Stay here with me. It will pass as these things do; it means nothing. Live your faith, Mary. Oh Mary! If you go to them now it is over. Do you want that? Is that what you want?" She almost shouted it, although our faces were but inches apart.

"Yes, Naomi. That is what I want. I choose now to end this deception, for the grieving is worse in the holding off."

She saw my resolve deepen as it had long ago, when the men had come to stone me. She opened her arms to me and I went into them. We held each other for a long moment.

And Naomi said, "Mary, it will all pass away. Remember. Remember that you love one unto the other from your souls. Nothing else matters."

Her face, so ancient and dear, bent unto me, calling forth my truth, speaking to me of divine justice and of the choice to remember the design. But I was in the grief of the web of illusion and heeded her not. I held her tightly, but I had not within me solace to give her.

I ran into the darkness to face Judas and Martha.

I found them together in the night, and I knew he had been seduced.

I knew that he was under her spell and that the time had come for the parting. I had known and yet denied it at the same time, because I knew what it meant, and I was trying to put off the leaving.

They looked up at me without guilt on their faces, although the one my sister was bedding was Judas, my earthly husband, the father of my children.

They looked at me with triumph and scorn, my sister with a vainness and a haughtiness that he had chosen her over me, that she had won.

He looked at me with repleteness, saying with the look that here was someone he was equal to and with whom he was treasured and special.

Their eyes betrayed me, both sets of eyes, looking at me with a hatred that burned holes through my body.

Love scorched me, for it had turned upon itself and laughed at me for having believed in it.

I turned away, looking at them no longer, and went to gather my things.

When I returned, Naomi helped me to pack the cloths which she had made for me and those few belongings she knew I would want. And as I was doing, she set her resolve and thought not of the future.

But as she knelt to pack my things, her hands were shaking and suddenly wet, and she knew that tears fell from her eyes.

And as we said good-bye, her heart made no sound but the beating of time through the walls of her grieving.

THE FINAL PARTING

Judas and I stood looking one to the other.
Words of grief and anguish lay between us
as something dead, something we had killed.

And we had killed something.
We had killed the reality of happiness we had lived for so
many years together.

It was not because he had lain with my sister, but because it was time for
him to find the truth within himself. And it was time for me to learn to be
alone. Perhaps one and the same learning after all.

I was reluctant to look at his eyes, the eyes of the one who seemed to
betray me.

I felt like death.

I wished that the pain I felt had killed me completely, instead of killing
only my joy.

And now, there were no more words.
They had been spoken as spears to maim and to kill, and I could not
believe that we had created it, because we knew the design. It was only
that we needed to be apart, not that we needed to kill our love or hurt
the other.

I wondered why it was so hard for us to do it gently and reasonably, why there must be pain and ego and judgement.

He had been my best friend, and I knew he was still. But for now we were to be apart, the friendship gone. We would remember each other only in grief because we had not chosen to be completely honest and fulfill our love through truth.

I wondered again why the design called for the parting.
Yet I knew the answer in the same instant, for there was no other way for him to find himself.

He must be alone until he found himself.

And I must go and find Christ and help him to pass.
I must live my humbleness, going from place to place, asking for the bread of the day and finding a place to abide in the night.

I must give my knowing and help to protect the knowledge so that it would remain within the land after we had gone.

Judas was bitter. My sister had told him many things that were untrue about me and about us. She had altered the truth, and he was confused, feeling me now as different from him, as though we had never been the same flesh and the same blood and the same being.

I thought of the children that he had fathered and I had carried, of the places we had built to house them, and the miles we had traveled to find safety. As the years passed there were so many memories, beautiful and whole and joyful—until she had found us.

It had been gradual. She was clever, and I had grown more afraid, and therefore, more distant. I had not left physically but had withdrawn because I was afraid and knew what was to come. She had moved to fill the void which he felt within him, for we had always shared the energy, Judas and I, one to the other, being as two, the one. And he had grown closer to her in my absence.

I did not blame him, for to him I had gone away. He did not realize, would not realize until I was gone, that her loving him in this way was an illusion, as was his loving her.

He would be alone on the mountain before the truth fully met his mind, and then it would be too late. I would be gone, and he would know what he had done, and what he had to face, and that he had to be alone for the rest of his life. There would be none other to take my place. . . or to take the place of his quest for himself.

He would look, though, and seek feeling in others, loving them in the ways of the flesh. But never would he find what he sought. I mourned for this and loved him more in this instant. Yet now as he faced me, he was arrogant and defiant and still vindictive, as if he had what he sought, as though our connection was already severed, and he was free.

I felt again the pain of that severing.

He had wanted to be free of the design. All this time he had equated me with the design, had confused the two, believing that he needed to run from me, and then he would be free of the design. Now it all made sense, for why else would he have wanted to be separate?

He believed that I was the cause of his pain, that I sustained it and brought it home to him. He was tired of running, tired of being the scapegoat, tired of what he had done and what he had not done, and tired of the people, forever trying him and hanging him and judging him in their minds.

And rather than sharing his pain with me, he began to withdraw into his own inner chamber of torture, and there were more and more women and more and more longings for joyful nights to ease the pain.

I watched him change from the one I had known to one tortured. It was reinforced by the outer illusion, and there was no one but me who knew the truth.

So he retreated, as I had, until the pathways were confused and the communication muddied, and the language did not say what we needed it to say. I wondered if I could have changed the design. If I had stayed, if my fear had not brought me to the place of withholding, would my sister have been able to come between us?

Suddenly, I wanted to be gone—wanted to leave this moment in time and move on, because it was my only salvation. If I stayed, or followed him, or begged him, I would betray myself. Since we could not meet halfway, there was nothing left to do. I had to go.

So I took a deep breath, feeling a pain shoot through my center, cutting me in half. A part of me longed to die, and yet I knew I must stay and find Christ, for I had more work to do. But I was so tired, so weary.

The human part of me that loved Judas fell away, dying slowly, dying, dying. I reached into the pain and sent out for the light, for I knew if I did not, I would harbor the pain and it would begin to kill my life force and diminish my spirit.

I called upon the consciousness of Christ, and I surrounded myself in light. In Judas' eyes, it was my final mistake. The final act which rendered us separate, and gave him permission to believe in his choice.

For he saw me transcending the pain and leaving him, and he was angered. I reinforced his belief that I was better and holier, and he, darker.

I had done it because I knew it was the way, knew he had the same choice and the same ability.

He chose not to follow me into light.

There was nothing else for me to do.

I said to him the words:
>"Remember that you are a part of the divine plan.
>Remember that the 'illusion' of the world
>is not the truth;
>Remember that you are trusted beyond
>measure—Remember!"

The words came to him through me, but not from me. The ones with no names had come upon me, and I spoke the words to him from them so that he would know the truth of his calling.

It was his time of rendering. He was given an opportunity to choose: light or dark, love or fear. And I saw him choose fear, his head lifting back in that arrogance which masked the aloneness.

All that was left was to speak to him from the truth of our soul's oneness which had brought us to this moment, so I did.

>"There will come a time when we will love again, you and I,
>and all that has gone before will remain.
>It will remain between us, causing us mistrust, one to the other.
>We will continue, life after life, time after time, until finally, we
>come into the light of our calling.
>We will find each other again, and my sister will come to you again;
>you will cast her aside, and we will learn to love and trust.
>We will be together again without pain, and without competition,
>and without mistrust.

"We will call out to each other through the time in between until
we have affected the perfection of our unity together.
This is true, and it will stand the test of all time because we will
prove together that love never dies. We will prove this together, and
it is designed and will be affected, regardless of the turning."

I spoke it with conviction to him and to myself.
I spoke it with conviction to the mountains, and the desert, and the valleys,
and to the sky, and the stars, and the moon which reflected now on the
skins of our bodies.
I spoke it to the heavens and to the gateway, and I was affirming it and
requesting it and bequeathing it, all at once.
I charged him to remember it through the calling, and I looked at him
again, planting my face and my body and our memory within his deepest
knowing, his deepest core.

And I whispered, "I will love you through all time."
Then, looking one last time into his eyes, I turned, walking away from him
into the night, carrying those things I had brought so long ago, the time
when I had left Israel.

A wolf howled, a hawk circled, and the crows cawed to mark the passing.
For we had again begun a new chapter, and this was the last.
This was the last.

I mounted my burro and, without looking back, rode off alone into the night.

If I had looked back, I would have seen Judas hold out his arm to me, but I did not. I only set my resolve and turned my thoughts to what I had yet to accomplish and prayed for the courage to live the design.

My Third Turning

A Tribute To Saschai

I traveled the Earth at night with my burro, Saschai.
I talked to her as we followed the land and the pathways, seeking the places where our calling would find its reward.

She was constant and loyal and made me smile.
Her ears were long and soft, her fur rich and deep.
She kept me warm in the cold and made noises in the night to keep the wild creatures away.

I was closer to her now than to anyone else, for I was alone.
I loved the people and was with them almost every day, and yet I knew there was a part of me that needed to be away from them, that needed to be apart.

I did not stay in any one place for long, knowing that my work was to travel to as many of the people as possible. Their homes could not really be my home, for I must keep on the journey until it was done, finding solace within myself.

Saschai followed me in the day as I attended the people, and she would make her sounds near me, reminding me that she was there. She understood my calling, and since she was alone also, we shared the aloneness as sisters.

At the close of the day, after supping, she would come to me, and I would feed her and say farewell to the people. We would depart as the sun spoke to the night and called it out, sleeping together on the Earth.

She was my friend, and as we traveled, we would settle into each other, my form becoming her form, riding the miles as one.

She knew that we journeyed to India, always aware of the calling of Christ to whom we were drawn. We spoke of him in the way of humans and creatures, and she knew him from the images in my mind, feeling his essence.

She was constant, her presence a gift to me, her loyalty touching me deeply and making me thankful. And so I cherished her greatly, for she was all that I had.

THE BIRTHING

I rode swiftly, urging Saschai onward into the cool, damp darkness of the midnight sky, for I heard the calling in my mind and answered it.

There was one, a woman, coming into her time, and I must be there to assist her. The cycles and the rhythms of her birthing were unbalanced, and the body and the soul of the unborn child were, as yet, disconnected.

If there was no one to bond the spirit to the body at birth, the soul would have no grounding place and would bind to the mother and to the patterns of man, and the beliefs of fear and judgement.

This was a special soul, one who would help to lead the people after I had gone, and it had been appointed that I attend it. I would teach it the ways of the Earth and reinforce the pathways of its calling, and that was why I must assist in its coming forth.

I was almost there. I could feel the energy of the coming, calling me forward.

When I arrived, I took my pack from Saschai and left her to graze, knocking upon the door frame of the small home before me.
The mother answered the knock, not appearing surprised to see me, relieved at my presence. She remarked that she was alone now. Her man, a shepherd, had gone with his flock, and she said it was good that I was there to be with her.

She was older and seasoned, her face rich with experience and tempered with time, and this was her first birthing.

She invited me within and we sat in the way of women. I listened to her passage. She told me of the days of her life and the ways of her learnings, and I was aware of her fears and her strengthenings.

After a time she relaxed, telling me of her dreams, and then finally, of her saddenings.

At times we laughed together, but always quietly and softly, as if honoring the presence of the unborn child through the whispers of our caring.

And after a time, when I knew that she was ready to listen to me, I told her of why I had come.

I reached within me to the core of my memory and began to speak:

> There is a place called the Hierarchy
> where there is no hatred or fear or judgement,
> the place of the source, from which all souls are born.
>
> The truth is born with us from this space also;
> the truth of who we are and where we are from and why we have
> come here to learn.
>
> But we forget this.

When we are born on the Earth, if those who birth us do not
tell us of this truth, we do not remember it.
And therefore an amnesia is born and we feel separation from the
truth and from the Gods.

The ways of humankind, the greed, the fear, and the judgement, are
because we do not remember that we are all from the same place,
that we are all the same.

The forgetting causes pain and then, after a time,
the pain is expected.
When the children are born,
they are taught that
the pain is a part of life,
and that the separation is a part of life,
and the competition
and the fear
are a part of life.

And then, sometimes, there are souls born who come to the Earth
to help the people remember the truth.
Your child is such a one.

I paused a moment and let the words stand between us, giving her time to
take in what I had said.

After a moment, I continued:

> Your child will be a girl.
> She will remember what the people have forgotten and will teach them. She brings hope and will speak to them of the truth and the oneness which they seek.
>
> She will remember that she is one with the Gods and will act as such, healing and standing as a guide to the people on their inner journey.
>
> She will help the people remember that they are divine, that they are light, and that they come from the truth and will return to the truth.

I stopped my speaking and rose to add wood to the fire. Then I moved the water to the heat and began preparing some steepened brew.

I did so to give her time, for the tears were standing as droplets unshed in her eyes, and her memory was stirring, but not yet ripe.

"Why do you tell me this?" she asked.

"I tell you this because of the child," I answered.
"As she is born, it is important that she remain at one with the Hierarchy and the Earth at the same time. This will help her remember."

I paused and then continued.

"During her first years it will be necessary to teach her and to remind her so that she knows her calling and remembers who she is and what she has come to do."

She waited, as if weighing her words before she spoke.
"I am seasoned, as you know," she said.
"I have wondered for these months of my confinement why, now, I would conceive to bear a child. My husband and I, for many years, have had no life between us, and now. . . ."

She paused, looking away from my eyes, and then, after a while, meeting them again.

"Is it so?" she asked.

I heard the unspoken questions between us.

She wanted to know if her destiny was tied to the unborn child and if bearing her would help to bring a change in the ways of the world.

She asked me if the child was her contribution to the unity of which I had just spoken and if she could find this unity through the passage of her calling into motherhood.

She asked the question each mother asks silently before that moment of birthing. "Can what I now create bring the love and unity I have sought but been unable to find?

"Can I love this child enough to change the patterns of what is and create here what I know can be?"

She asked me if the world could change and if there could be love and if there could be acceptance, and peace, and the remembering.

As I heard her questions, I knew I had asked them also, as does each woman at the moment of procreation, and I answered her very softly, "Yes."

We looked at each other then in complete understanding, and I said, "It is time to begin."

She nodded and moved slowly and deftly to the stove where she finished preparing a brew of strong herbs and leaves to see us through the long night to come.

I watched her as she made me a small meal of bread and figs and meat. As she moved, I saw that she was more assured, the fear gone— a new determination showing in the carriage of her body and within her womanness.
It stirred me deeply, for it affirmed my calling, and I was well rewarded.

I let her prepare the food even though she was beginning her rhythm and the cycle of birth was upon her. This was the only way she could repay me, and it was a point of honor between us.

She gave to me the food, and I ate what she had prepared.

She nodded to me then and said, "I am now ready."

I began to speak.

> The child is now moving into the tunnel.
> The vibrations of density from the Earth are now affecting her
> memory, and she is seeing only the light, forgetting the calling, and
> where she is, and why she is moving through the dimensions.

I paused and drank some brew and felt the knowing come into the
mother, and then I continued.

> The pattern of destiny is encoded into the soul, but for the child to
> remember it, she must be connected again to the memory as
> she is born.

> I can do this for a time, but it is your calling to instill the knowledge
> of divinity and the memory of her origin into the consciousness of
> your own child.

> When the child's soul is honored and upheld from the time of birth,
> there is much joy, for there is no experience of separation from the
> knowledge and the unity within. The child is happy, well contented,
> fulfilled within, needing nothing in the way of the human to
> give her dignity or self-worthiness.

The child creates from the inner potential and remembers
her design. When this memory is real to the child, she has a
sense of belonging and knows the angels as well as her physical
playmates. The world is a beautiful place of discovery and creation.
This is the way of the calling.

"How can I do this for my child?" she asked.

Close your eyes and place your thoughts in the seed of light in the
center of your body, in the place where your ribs come together in a
point. There, yes, right below the heart.

Breathe there, and you will feel your knowing.

Ask that your light and the light of your child now be one.

Imagine a light in the place where you hold the child in the womb.

Now, as you feel and remember unity, expand your thinking to be a
part of the light which your child brings. Feel your lights as one.

Yes. Now as the rhythms and cycles of the child are felt in your
body, you will feel the quickening more strongly, and the time
between cycles will be shorter. Stay at one with the soul of the
child now, and the birth will be easy and quick and clear.

We moved to the place which had been prepared for the birthing, and
I continued to instruct her in the breathing and the merging.
I told her I was also bonding with the child, and we continued for some
time, feeling the soul of the child approaching now, more completely.

I instructed her to breathe into the light of the union between her
and the child and to form a bridge of this light between her womb
and the outside world. This would lead the child through the canal
and into the world in light.

I asked her to keep the image of light inside and outside of her body
at the same time, so that the child would see no separation and
would be born in unity, remembering that the universe is a safe
place to be.

Just before she was born, I sent out the call to the child and anchored
universal light in her consciousness helping the mother to bridge the
span between dimensions.

I showed the child the light of her calling and led her out of the womb into
the density of Earth affirming her divinity:

> "You are spirit, and so you shall remain," I said over and over again.
> "Your truth shall be honored here.
> You are free to create from the design within and live your potential
> and hold to the memory of your knowing."

When the mother had fulfilled the birthing, and the cleaning and ordering had been accomplished, we sat, the three, and bonded the light between us once again.

I instructed her, and she began the ritual of the birthing of light into form.

She began connecting her seed with her child's seed again, feeling the bond between them.

She then brought light into the top of the child's head and drew it through the small body, creating a waterfall with the light. She did this several times until she felt the light steady and constant throughout her child's body.

She then took the child's small feet in her hands and held the bottoms saying slowly and distinctly:

> "You have chosen to come into form.
> You have chosen to come into form.
> You have chosen to come into form.
>
> I anchor you into the mother Earth.
> I anchor you into the mother Earth.
> You have chosen this form.
>
> You are light.
> You are light.
> You are light.

"You are light and light you shall remain.
You are light and light you shall remain.
You are light and light you shall remain."

She said the words of the affirmation to her child with intent. Then she placed one hand on her heart and the other hand on her baby's heart, speaking in the child's ear and saying:

"The bond that we have is through love;
what I teach you I teach from love;
what is not of your truth,
I give you permission to release.

I acknowledge your divinity and your spirit.
You have arrived on the planet Earth, and you
are a part of our family.
Know that you are creative and can achieve and
accomplish anything that you desire and that there are
no conditions on my love for you.

I will love you, always, without question."

As she finished the ritual of the birthing, she drew the child to her breast and they continued the joining.

Since she was more open in the first forty-eight hours after her birthing than at any other time in her life, I told her it was important to run the light of spirit through her body before she held the infant so that she would be filled with light when she held her. I also spoke of the need for her to be with her own spirit, while cherishing the bond with her child.

I instructed the mother to spend some moments each day joining with her child's seed of light and going with the child into the light of the Hierarchy and the place of truth. Since the first twenty-four months establishes the foundation between the hemispheres of consciousness, I told her that every day for two years the child would need to hear an affirmation that she is light.

I stayed with them for six months following the birthing.
Each day I instructed the mother and sent the child a validation of her purpose and spoke to her the affirmation of light.

I grew to love the girl child and her mother, and we spent many hours talking, sharing, and loving.

I told the mother of the future of the child and gave her the teachings of the soul to share with her when she was older:

> To always uphold the creativity of the child and
> encourage her uniqueness, affirming her child's divinity daily.

> To listen every morning to her child's dreams and, at night before
> bed, to listen to the experiences the child had that day.

This would help to integrate the unconscious and
conscious processes of the child every twenty-four hours.

To have the child express all of her feelings without
judging them and to give the child an example of this
through her own honest expression of emotion.

This would explain the ways of the world and the laws of man,
telling her why things are as they are.
This would give her the understanding necessary to live
here and respect others. If the child respected the ways
of others, then others would respect her ways.

I spoke to the mother about the Earth as a learning place and about
the lessons the child's soul had come to learn. I told her to teach
the child that the lessons did not have to be learned through pain
because pain is man-made and is not created from the Gods.

I instructed her and the child in the ways of the heart:
To love unconditionally,
To ask for the memory of the design,
To join daily with the seed of light of those you love,
To spend some moments together in dreaming and being.

I stayed because of my calling, yes, but also because it was a respite from
the travel and the aloneness of my outer existence.

I explored the hills and the valleys there and took the child with me, explaining to her about the Earth and the elements and the force fields. We went into the wind and the rain and under the trees and the stars. We touched the living things of the Earth every day, and the child learned about life.

And as I was preparing to leave, I told the child about the truth within her, telling her of why she had come and of why I must go. I spoke to her as if she were of my years, sometimes using my tongue and sometimes using my mind.

She would listen, now barely sitting by herself, propped against the rocks beside her earthly home.
She had clear almond eyes which reflected the memory of her inner truth and the knowledge within her soul.
She was happy, smiling often, and content to be here.

When it was finished, we stood together in the door frame, the three as one—one in our calling, one in our being, one in our intention as women to create the wave of truth.

I knew we had done well and I smiled, kissing them on each cheek.

I mounted Saschai then and rode forward, even now feeling the next calling. I was going in a direction, a direction which would bring me to Christ, for we had so appointed it.

It would take many Earth years, and yet I did not sigh, for I was well contented. There was no place of lack within.

The child had filled me again with the presence of home, and it was fresh in my memory, as was the image of the prophecy and light the child had chosen to bring to the Earth.

As I rode away, the sun came over the mountain, and all the memories of all of the sun's risings came with it.

TOGETHER AGAIN

I began to feel Christ as I approached the cave in the hill.

We had made this assignation so long ago, before the turning with Judas and before my long journey, and I knew he would be here.

I felt my love for him as I drew nearer, the feelings I had shut away rising within me. And with them rose the pain of the separation now that it was over, the separation from him and from Judas. It tore at me as it had not before, tore at the hardness in my heart where I had sealed it to protect myself.

Suddenly the sorrow and the joy were one within me, no longer distinct but married, one fulfilling the other, the joy I felt at this reunion and the sorrow I had lived in its absence.

I wondered again at the design. Judas and I had grown apart because our intention to love was not enough. Love must be honored and valued above all things, and we had not done this. Our fear was stronger than our love, creating separation.

Christ and I were separate physically, yet our love had deepened through the space of our absence, and I could feel him calling me to him.

I would meet him now and we would travel together for nine years, binding within the Earth the knowledge and light Christ carried, until the time when the people would honor themselves and the Earth as their mother, acknowledging the divinity and the sacredness of all things.

And my life? What did it mean? The words the people were spreading had reached me already. Their judgement had made me the whore, had twisted the truth.

For what had I lived if the truth of my knowing would never be acknowledged? In 2000 years all would be known.
2000 years. . . and where would I be then?
So much to undo, so many to tell of the truth.

The human part of me could not accept and understand it fully, so I turned away from the questions and began to send my light to Christ.

I urged Saschai onward, and she responded quickly, feeling my nervous excitement. I saw him then, in the distance, standing with one hand over his brow, searching the horizon. He stood still as he saw me, waving his other hand, waiting for me. As I came closer I saw his smile, his eager eyes upon me, intently searching within me, desiring to know me again. His body was lean and fine, his heart strong and open unto me.

Saschai was excited now for she smelled his scent and knew who he was, and she hurried forward. He was aware of her, sensing her excitement. As I came beside him, he took her head and stroked her mane as he stood looking up at me.

We stayed that way for a moment, the excitement building, neither one moving or speaking, saying the words with our hearts and eyes instead.

Then he let Saschai go and held his arms up to me, and I went into them.

He said nothing except, "My Mary, my Mary," over and over in the way that I remembered so well. He held me so closely that our bodies fused, and I stopped thinking and controlling and let go, allowing the merging.

He felt every moment of the fifty years of our separation. The moments I had lived were reflected in the pathways of his vision, and I did not stop them. I let him see them completely. I felt him transform them, infusing the pain and aloneness with light and joy, and then with understanding. I was clear and soft, the understanding releasing the darkness within me, making it light.

Then I felt Christ fully, and we relived all the memories of all the times of our love, and I was breathless, holding him and opening to him and reaching into him, all at the same time. He held me and opened unto me and reached into me also. The moment was indelible through time, enfolding us totally.

Then I watched the images which he played upon my vision of the days of his journey. We had lived lives of parallel experience: teaching the people to remember the truth, healing and birthing them, inspiring their potential, loving them for their essence, helping them to die. One by one we had come together with their souls, anchoring the light and truth into their knowing.

Now we were together to anchor that truth and light into the Earth so that it would be here for the time when the people would remember, 2000 years in the future.

He continued to hold me, and I, him. I felt myself relax and the puzzles fade. The searching ceased, and I was at peace.

Then I said, "Your mother? What of your mother?"

He said to me then, very gently, "My Mary, my mother lies in the cave beyond us." He turned and raised his arm, showing me the cave in the hill.

"She is ready now to make her way through the pathways to the Hierarchy, and waits to speak words with you before she goes. She has done well, coming here to end her days in the peace of the valley of the eagles. She has been of great help to me in these last years."

I felt her then, as I had not before, and knew she had shielded her presence from me to give us time to be alone and to reunify. She had given me the time I needed to heal the wounds of my calling.

I loved her so much in that moment, for she was one who inspired love. Even as she passed she was giving, thinking of ways to cherish and uphold others.

I kissed him then, quickly, and ran toward the cave.

She was waiting for me, lying propped against the wall near the cave's entrance, sunlight falling upon her body. She had always loved the warmth and sought the sun, and I knew I would find her such.

Her body was wizened and tiny now that her force of life was diminished, and her eyes reflected the choice of her soul to leave the body.

She was cheerful still. She loved her life and she loved me; this was apparent in the smile which she bestowed upon me as I entered the cave.

The richness of our weaving as sisters was upheld now by our hearts as we clung together sharing the images and visions of the times we had been apart, just as Christ and I had done a short while before at our reunion.

The Mother said to me, "Mary, will others live the richness of the lives we have accorded, or experience as much the difficulty? Will what we live create the outcome we seek?" I had asked the questions she now asked and knew she spoke of the calling: knowing the truth and living the light in this place of Earth, where joy and despair are woven as the fabric of human existence.

Her question, rhetorical, brought to us a vision. I saw a crystal ball turning endlessly within the center of her outstretched hand. In the crystal was the past, the present, and the future, and she showed me her capacity in that moment as sorceress, magician, and shaman.

She showed me the pathways, and I attended her. In her outstretched palm the ball of fine crystal appeared and disappeared spontaneously. Within the crystal were the lives of the players of the design. As I watched, our pathways spun together and apart, and I saw them clearly.

She showed me all the lives, or points of reality, and all the identities, and I knew as I watched that she gave me a great gift. She offered to me the future so that I could have resolution for all time.

So I asked the spinning ball to show me specifically my pathway with Judas and with Christ and with the other players.

I saw my future and my past resolving my present through time. I saw her and who she would be when we met again and how I would know of her and what we would be together. With each of the players I saw my future and my past and my present.

Then she showed me the answers to the questions I had asked on my journey that morning—the questions about truth and the people and the future.

What I saw inspired my faith in the outcome. At first the crystal showed me fear that was strong and people who maimed and killed one another. It showed poisons on the Earth and in the waters. It would be thousands of years before there would be peace on Earth or in my garden.

Then one day the light would call forth the truth, and the people would remember and choose to live in peace, and all would be accorded.

The visions made the understanding come forth to sit with the memory, and then the crystal ball faded, and we were alone with the moment.

I knew then that she had been with me that morning and on other mornings, even when I did not feel her presence.

410

She had sent me the light to help me remember my calling and support my turnings. In all the times of my growing she was there, near to me when I needed her, as if she knew what would transpire and how she could help me.

And she spoke then, saying,
"My daughter, you are to me a precious jewel, a girl-child such as none other. If I had not loved your mother so profoundly, I would have taken you when you were but just born to raise with Christ."

She laughed softly, and I saw the image in her mind of the first time she had seen me in the arms of my mother.

She had christened me before the men of the temple had seen me. Before my father, the rabbi, had honored me in the way of the temple, she had honored me in the way of the Goddess. I carried the mark of the cross and the star and the houses of men and of the Gods, long before they were known by the people, and she thus baptized me, so that I would not forget who I was and the lineage I carried during my earthly journey.

Then I remembered how she had sojourned to me when I was in my twelfth year, at the time of my blooming, the time of my coming forth as a woman.

With the memory I felt a rush of warmth, and a flush crossed my cheeks. She looked at me, and knowing what I was thinking said,
"Speak to me of your blooming, Mary."

And as I told her the story I recalled:

It was a beautiful spring day, on the eve of my twelfth birth day. My mother told me that there would be a surprise for me and that this was a day that I would remember always. She told me to bathe and gave me a plain white robe to wear that I had never seen before. She assisted me in dressing, which was very strange, for my mother never assisted me in dressing, now that I was almost a woman.

But this day she stayed beside me, attending me and my hair and my cloth. I felt her love strongly but differently, and yet I did not know how it was different. She helped me, and yet I knew that she did so to be with me and to have a reason to stay at my side. She was nervous—not for herself, but for me. And yet, I did not know why.

As we finished with the dressing and prepared to begin the day, she said a very strange thing to me. She looked at me very intently with those dark, starlit eyes, and said, "Tonight you will know who I am, Mary, and you will know who you are, and you will know who all women are."

Then she held me for one brief moment to her soft form, gathering me quickly to her and then, as quickly, setting me aside.

Before I could question her about what she meant, the Mother of Christ arrived. She was my mother's favorite friend and one of my favorite friends also. And after we had all kissed on two cheeks and looked into each other's eyes, we sat together and talked.

After a time my mother withdrew, leaving us alone.

The Mother then asked me to walk with her into the land beyond the village, and so we walked there together.

Inside her wide belt she carried grains and herbs, rocks and water, earth and crystals, and a wand. Over her shoulder was a richly woven cloth, and she found a place under a huge olive tree and laid the cloth before her on the ground inviting me to sit upon it.

Then one at a time, she took from her wide belt the elements she carried, and she gave them to me as a gift to mark my becoming, telling me of their essence and their power.

Then she pulled forth the wand from her belt and held out her hand. I put mine within hers, and she placed the wand within my fingers and closed my hand.

She said, "The power has come to you now, and the power will go from you again. Know that the power is, and there is no time when the power is not. Remember this, and it will assure your place in the kingdom of heaven."

She lay me down on the cloth then and gently placed her hand on my body, moving from part to part, speaking to me from her wisdom. This is what I remember:

She began by placing her hand on the top of my head, saying, "Here is where the Gods speak to you. I call them forth to sit upon your shoulder and guide you in the world."

She then placed her hand on my forehead and said,
"All things are visible to you here, seen and unseen. I call forth your vision to show you the way."

At my throat, she said,
"Here is the place where you can speak the truth: I call you to speak from truth, live from truth, and act from truth always."

She touched both of my breasts at one moment and said,
"Here is where men will touch you and babies will suckle you: I call forth the milk of honey from the fluids of the universe to nourish your woman-truth through all time." I began to feel passion in my body, and she smiled and told me we were birthing it together, and she said,
"Never be afraid to love. The places of the body are for pleasure and nurturing, for you and others. Men and women equally will love you, and you must live only with the moment, not with rules designed to control your pleasure and your love. Live only from the *truth* of what is born from your knowing in each moment, and you will regret nothing, according joy in your life. Joy is felt when you are free to create in each moment the fullest choosing of that moment. Joy is the passageway to freedom and knowledge."

She moved her hands then to the bone in the middle of my chest between my ribs and said,
"Here is the seed of light where the people will remember their path to truth and accord you your place in the design.

"Know that they have the truth within them and that they will find it. See them always, Mary, as if they are remembering it, and know that what you do helps them such to do."

She then placed her hands on the center of my body and said, "This is where the potential is actualized to fulfill the self. I call forth your right to live your full potential in the world."

She then placed her hands on the lower part of my abdomen and said, "Here is where you will bring in and let out all ideas, thoughts, beliefs, and experiences of your entire lifetime. Remember that you will carry your children here, for this is their world before they are born. Always affirm here that you are in balance from the night and the day and in harmony with the fluids of the universe."

She then placed her hands on my feet and said, "Here is where humans walk and angels dance, and where the power of the Earth is given through the understanding of the heavens. Always honor your feet and the feet of those you love, for herein lies the divinity."

Then she placed her right hand on the place of womanness, between my legs, and her left hand she placed on my heart, and she said, "Know that you are clear and pure and that the light of all the Gods and Goddesses flows from you. The blood that you now will shed comes as a symbol of your right to bear life and to know the design and to remember the calling. It is the blood of your sisters and is your vow to be at one with them, regardless of the turning.

415

"If you do not uphold the calling of your womanhood and join in the heart with your sisters, you will have pain at the month of your bleeding and at the time of your birthing. Remember the joy of the fruits of your labor and call to you the sisters of your life and all lives, and they will be with you."

As she was speaking these words, my mother and my mother's sisters, and the women of the village and their friends, all older than their twelfth year, came around me.

It was now dark, and they lifted me and carried me, all surrounding me and supporting me, into the women's cave of darkness deep in the woods.

They had built a fire, and they lay me in the center of a circle of rocks and crystals, such as those the Mother had given me that day.

The crystals were of the colors of the rainbow, and the women taught me of them, and I learned where on my body each color lay and how to use the stones for healing.

I had never seen the women as this. They were solemn and quietly spoken in the world, and here they were full of the power and the calling. The darkness brought forth their light, and they were alive and joyful. They spoke with conviction and knowledge, and I felt safer than I had ever felt before.

And then I remembered that I was here to teach also and that this power would be given to Christ and that it was the women's rites that would balance his male power and this was why we were here, for the men and the women would be equal again one day both in the world and in the calling.

The women then began to take the cloths from my body and I acquiesced, feeling safe and warm and excited. For this was a ritual and I was here now, part of a rich fabric of love and tenderness, and I was honored and upheld, and it was a blessing.

The women gently stroked the length of my body with the wings of birds. Using feathers, they fanned the smoke of cedar and sage over me, removing the memories of the world and replacing them with the memories of the calling. They sang to me a lullaby of sisterhood, weaving the tones together high and low as a fabric which soothed my senses and caressed me. They poured oil over me, kneading my flesh gently and softly at first, and then more deeply, to call forth the memory of each cell and bring its perfection into my awareness.

I felt the power rise within me as a flame and a wave and I felt the soothing of it as a longing fulfilled.

They spoke to me as they touched my body and fanned the fire within me, calling it forward and releasing it, and calling it forward and releasing it again.

They built the memory and the fire and the power within me time after time, as if calling my womanness from a great distance and soothing its calling and firing it and soothing it, and then again they fired it.

They spoke to me then of passion and men and the ways of the world and the ways of the heart. They played images across my awareness of hearts and mouths and mergings, of men and women, and women and women, and men and men, and I knew the pictures, but did not know from where I knew them.

They showed me how to spark the longing and call forth the fire of desire and hold it within my body: to pulse and grow and overflow. They showed me with their minds the pictures of pleasure and its pathway, and they began kissing my body and touching me in the places of womanness. And this time they did not release the passion, but fueled it. I was carried on the waves of our visions into the worlds of stars and light and felt the merging deep within me of all worlds and all light; and it touched my form, and I became one with my body for the first time.

The stars lay their scent upon me and I made sound from my throat of love's pleasure, and my earthly mother brought the wand inside my body, and I bled my woman's blood, my sister's blood, my lover's blood.

I remember waves of light flowing up from between my legs and the place of my womb into my heart and finding a new peace here in my body, in this place of Earth.

And they stroked me and brought the fire to smoulder within me, and I grew calm and full of peace.

Then my sisters, young and old, bathed me in fresh water and herbs and washed my hair, touching me with the fragrance of the flowers. And when they had finished, we all lay together holding each other, as the sun rose outside of our dark cave.

And I knew that I was a woman.

In the cave, the Mother of Christ and I looked at each other and we did not speak. She chuckled finally, a soft sound of pleasure from her throat, and said, "You tell it very well."

I held her hand then and spoke to her of my gratitude and of the love I felt for what she had done for me all these many years. She listened and received my love and gratitude.

"I also have gratitude for you, Mary. You have borne children and you know, more than most, the pathway of women in this world. To know that you would be beside my son when I could not be with him, and to know that you would love him as yourself and protect him with your life, has made my life bearable, livable. The design accords us its plan, and then we must live it, but oh, so humanly.

"To reach inside and call the truth and see its beauty and to watch it
then be dissolved by fear; to have faith in the outcome and then to
see the reality overlaid with the illusion, as you know, takes great
courage. And I have lived it more fully and more profoundly because
of you. You are, in truth, my daughter; the daughter of all time.
And you are my sister; the sister of all time, and I accord you."

She paused, squinting at me as she often did to see me more clearly, and
then she said, firmly squeezing my hand,

"Stay with him Mary, for he is alone, and you are all that he has, as he is all
that you have. Be with him as you both desire, and leave the first calling,
the calling of Israel. Follow your hearts and your bodies, for you know it is
what you and I do best, and there is no reason now for the abstaining."

I was confused, but did not question her, for she was tired, the memories
and the words of parting heavy for her.

I straightened her fragile body, rubbing her feet, showing her through my
touch of my deep caring. I took water and anointed her head and called in
the ones with no names and raised her spirit up. And all her cells were
bathed in the pure crystalline light of the heavens, and the kingdoms
surrounded her in glory.

I rose to call for Christ to help me with her passing, but before I left her, I
touched the places of her body that she had touched for me. And just as
she had opened these places of power for me so many years ago, I closed
them now, for her, in the true way of our sisterhood.

MARTHA'S LEARNING

In the chill of the early spring dawn, I washed in the clear, brisk water of the mountain stream. The sun shone on my back and shoulders, affording me warmth. As I dried myself with a fresh cloth, I looked at my body. My skin reflected the years of my living, my hands and feet dark from the sun. I touched my flesh. My skin was soft and pliant, tender, smoothly supple. And my womanness came around me and I felt the fire within me. I remembered the pleasure of my body, the moments of the flesh.

I thought back to last night, Christ and I holding the other before we slept, sharing the details of our journeys, recreating our oneness through the sharing of our essence and our hearts. But it was not physical between us—the constraint still there—the calling of Israel remembered and honored—our oneness ethereal. And I missed the physical.

I missed Judas—his smile, the intentness of his gaze, the fire of his longing. The memory of the passion we had always shared flowed through me, the passion and the longing. I sighed, another time, another place.

Then I remembered Martha. Oh, to have it resolved. To end the distrust and bitterness.

The bubbling stream spoke to me, bringing me from my reverie. I heard its journey: joyful and light, free and clear, the molecules dancing, joined in union.

The water's clarity touched my soul, and I felt the place of sadness within me. The sadness called me to acknowledge it, reminding me that I could receive the gift of its knowing.

I asked the water to help me in the resolution of my pain with Martha. Immediately the water accorded me, carrying me on the pathway of vision to the mountains of France, to the valley where I had said good-bye to Judas.

The figure of a woman stood at the foot of the mountain, staring at the brilliant color of the autumn day. I saw that she watched a man, a man who trudged through the dense scrub at the mountain's base, climbing steadily.

And then I saw that the woman who watched was my sister Martha, and the man who climbed was my husband Judas. . . .

Martha clasped her arms around her body as she watched Judas climb the mountain.

He had left her. Judas had left her, and he had not looked back. She was fetching, still beautiful, but he did not look back. Her beauty meant nothing to him now.

The taste of the joy of revenge soured in her mouth as she watched the resolute steps of her lover taking him away from her forever.

If he had been going to Mary, to a woman, any woman, she would have understood—but to go away to be alone! She felt rage at the rejection, the pain of the loss, and the fear of aloneness, all at once.

She knew it was over, but there must be something she could do, someone to go to, someone that she could turn to for solace.

Yes, yes, there was a man, a man of the village. A man with no woman. She thought of him and the times of their meeting. He had no woman, and yes, he had watched her; even Judas had remarked on it.

She wrapped her arms about herself more tightly. Then her arms loosened slightly and she breathed more deeply, almost a sigh. But she watched still. If he looked back, perhaps there was still a chance.

Then she knew he would never look back, for she had never meant to him what Mary had meant—she had joined with him only in the flesh.

She saw herself as he had seen her, seducing him, tricking him, slyly grasping for what she had wanted with no concern for others.

And she was diminished.

She sighed then, and relaxing her arms, she turned, placing her back to Judas, to Mary, and to all that she had been.

She stole a look behind her to the man climbing the mountain. She longed to go with him—to find the solace he sought, for herself. But solace was not her friend, and she did not know where to find it.

As she made her way toward the village, toward the man there, she felt tears on her cheeks and did not know why. The sadness did not go away, but spoke the truth of what she had done: her betrayal of Mary, the knowing that she had used Judas. And to what end? They were all alone and apart and afraid.

She wished for forgiveness, but there was no one there to ask it of. She saw herself clearly then and knew that now she would ask for forgiveness only because she had to ask for it to feel better. The past—the past was dead anyway—of another time and place. There was only now and she had nothing.

She continued to walk toward the village. Only now, perhaps now was enough after all. There was this man.

She turned one last time. She did not see Judas on the mountain. He was gone. The only sound was the sighing of the wind through the trees and the birds crying in flight overhead.

Suddenly, she felt the moment open and saw the sunlight before her, and she knew that she could ask for forgiveness, and as she acknowledged this, she felt Mary and Judas with her. They were here with her now; she could feel them.

She fell to her knees and began to cry. She saw all her years and the pain she had caused to so many, and she knew that there was no going back, that if she was going to change things, she would have to do it now. They were with her now, and she could make things right.

And yet she hesitated, still thinking of the desires and the vanity and the passion of what she wanted. If only she could have what she wanted.

She heard a voice within her ask, "What is it that you want?" She was taken aback. She stopped thinking and listened to the question within. "What do I want," she asked of herself?

She stopped crying and listened, listened for the answer. If the question was within her perhaps the answer was also.
She waited, holding her breath.

Then she heard the answer as if from a long distance.
I want peace, the peace of knowing that I am loved and forgiven and accepted.

Gathering her courage, she whispered,
"I ask for peace and love and forgiveness."

She waited, but she felt only the asking; she was still cast out and unaccepted. So she took a breath again and broke through the ice of her withholding and said to the day around her, loudly:

"Mary and Judas, listen to me. I ask your forgiveness. I am sorry for what I have done. I ask you to forgive me." She paused, gathering her courage, "I ask you to love me and to accept me."

Her chest wrenched, and sobs shook her body. Then she felt waves of love from Mary and Judas and the forgiveness she had sought.

And she felt a solace she had never known before. Her heart opened, and her love flowed forth. Then she said aloud, "Mary, I love you. I have always loved you."

And she heard Mary saying, "I love you, my sister." There was love flowing back and forth at last—after all these many years!

And this knowing brought her the peace of love and acceptance she had always sought, the knowing that she was clear and clean and new, and different. Yes! She was different! The thought brought her joy.

She rose from her knees and did not think to look at the mountain as she squared her shoulders and lifted her head, setting off for her future with pride. The peace of her knowing smoothed the edges of her being.

Mary loved her, and she loved Mary, and that was the key to everything. Loving was the key to everything. The love and the solace sat together within her. She felt a softness, a warming within, and she relaxed, thinking of what she did want, thinking of what she truly wanted, and of who she really was.

For the first time in her life she was content. She began to feel her calling rise within her. She was excited, excited about herself. And in this moment she finally understood her sister. She knew why the people had come to Mary, knew what it was to live one's potential.
And the understanding brought her the knowing,
and this learning wove a pattern of union within her.

As the vision faded, the image of Martha remained before me, the solace she felt softening the contours of her face, her knowing coming to rest within her eyes and in her smile. And I felt my heart open unto her, and felt within me the bond of our sisterhood and the union of our souls in oneness.

JUDAS CLIMBS THE MOUNTAIN

Christ and I sat one morning under the fullness of the sky, soaking the rays of the sun deeply into our bodies.

We were running the balance of power between, our hands on the other's heart, bonding through our love and joining our hearts in union.

Christ's mother had made her passage a few days before, and we were alone for the first time in many years.

We were just beginning our work of prophesy and healing together and would journey to Kashmir to prepare for our physical passings.

It was lovely to be together. It brought forth the memories of Israel and our love's blooming. I recalled the first time we had sat such, the time I had called Christ from Capernaum, after I had first lain with Judas.

The memory of my life with Judas brought sadness to my heart, and again I saw our parting. My heart contracted, and Christ's hand moved slightly upon my chest, deepening his touch. His love reached out to enfold me.

He placed the pictures of Judas in my awareness, showing me our times together and what we had learned. I relaxed into his hand and watched the images he placed in my mind. He showed me the words and the actions of both our pathways, and I saw them resolve in the unfolding. Christ then spoke of Judas and his choice for resolution, and the images shifted from past to present, and Christ showed me Judas.

I breathed deeply, feeling the pain finally lift as I saw the choice Judas was making—the choice of Judas to climb the mountain.

Judas felt the pulsing of the Earth beneath his feet as he climbed the mountain. With each step he felt her presence more distinctly, the subtle blending of the dew, the song of the birds, and the sunlight through the fog of the early morning. In his heart he cried out to her, his first mother, his real mother, the Earth. He had longed for her and for her nurturance, seeking it in the world, forgetting that what he sought was of the Earth and not of the world.

Climbing this mountain was a symbol to him of his life, and when he reached its peak, he was going to stop: to rest, to live, and to die.

He was going no further, only to the top of the mountain. He did not know how long he would live there, but he knew he would be alone. He would have no one, no one.

The thought frightened him. He had spent much of his life seeking to be with others because being alone frightened him. He thought of this for a moment as he made his way up the mountain. What had he been searching for? What was he afraid of? He knew that in his fear he had hidden from himself, had sought safety in the company of others, especially women.

Women—the women seemed safe. They reminded him of his first mother, the Earth, and he knew their ability to nurture and to sustain. They were at one with procreation and with the sensuality of the vine. They wove their being tenderly throughout their lives in the ways of their sisterhood.

He had tried so many times to be at one with them. What was he seeking, after all? What did they have, these women, that he craved and lusted after? What did they have? What did they represent?

His thoughts brought him again to his climb. Rocks and grass grew upon the mountain, and he felt them beneath his feet as he made his way. It was steeper here, the climbing more difficult. His weight was not balanced and he stumbled on a rock, falling to his knees.

He felt embarrassed, tricked by the Earth. He blamed the rock for his pain. As he knelt there he looked at the rock. It sat there just as it had before he came to rest upon it. He realized then that the rock had not caused his pain. He had caused his pain.

Magdalena had not caused his pain, and all of the women and all of the people had not caused his pain. He had caused his own pain. He had been out of balance—out of balance with the ability to nurture himself, to create, to sustain himself in harmony.

The Earth was still in the early morning and did not reply to his questions or his answers. She was there in balance, reflecting to him the current of life, sustaining herself through the fiber of being, not through seeking or questioning.

Being. Seeking was not being, and he had always sought.
Aggressively, aggressively.
His mind played for him the images of his seeking. He placed his head in his hands, and his anguish was felt more deeply than tears.

God, why? What have I done? Magdalena is now gone, my children have left me. My lovers are but illusions of merging and oneness, and here I am again, alone.

God did not answer him directly.

He waited there for what seemed a long time, until the sun was very hot upon his body. Then he opened his eyes.
Before him was a shimmering, a shimmering of light.
Lights were shimmering before his eyes.
He watched, unable to move or think, just watching.
There before him was a vision, distant and vague—unearthly.
He heard himself in the vision saying over and over again,

"I will find myself. There will be no one else.
When he is gone, I will have to find myself!!"

His heart stopped beating, and he held his breath. The vision became memory, and he knew where he had spoken these words before.

He thought of Christ and of what they had done together and of the design and of Magdalena. Then all of the pieces of his soul's pattern came into focus. He saw the vision resolve as he heard the words again.

"There will be no one else. When he is gone, I will have to find myself!!"

And then he heard the reply of the ones with no names, saying, "Yes, and in so doing, find him again."

With the acknowledgment came resolution. He held out his hands to the light and saw Christ there in front of him. The light was blinding his eyes, and so he closed them. The last thing he saw was the light shining into the darkness of his pain and the recognition that in finding himself, he had found Christ. And in the finding was the fiber and the vine, and the self, and the God, and all.

And he was at peace.

And as we felt his peace, Christ and I gathered together our light to make the reckoning full, resolving with Judas what he and I had not finished in the world.

THE FIELD OF GOLDEN GRASS

It was a crisp April day. The sun was strong now and urged us onward, our feet following the worn tracks of the animals, making our passage more easy. We were tired, and the winter snows were forcing us to find a place of comfort and rest. So we continued onward, searching, searching.

We were in the mountains called Himalayas, climbing down now into the valley, searching for a place to sojourn for the spring. The land called us forth, and we went without question, knowing that the place of respite awaited us.

We continued to walk, I in the lead, following the path which descended before us. At the base of the mountain was a ravine, a deep cleft of trees and jagged rock. Above it rose a snow-covered peak, marking the end of the valley. Ahead was a glacier, etched against the sky, stark and beautiful, the chill wind whirling the snow from its edges.

To the right was a field of golden grass. I stopped in mid-step. What was there about this field? A memory?

I quickened my pace as the path descended beside the ravine. Near the last incline a stream crossed in front of us, and at the bottom of the track I saw clearly the golden field of grasses and I knew that this was why we had come.

I hurried directly toward the field, leaving the others, feeling excitement overlaying my weariness; my need to walk in this field was as strong as my need for air. A longing drew me and soothed me all at once, the sacredness of this place filling me with the memory of home. They let me go first, my loved ones, knowing the joy would be sweeter if I were alone to savor it.

My eyes filled suddenly with tears as I remembered my connection to this place of golden grass. Here was a knowing, a recognition, a feeling of protection and sanction. Hallow and sacred, it called to me. It was a place of wisdom—a window through time to the dimension of spirit—where the veil was thin and the magic near.

I looked at the flat, protected area. It was warmer here, the wind still, the softness of the land reaching into the air and filling it. The scene before me was immense, every direction diverse yet synthesized, creating perfection the mind would not have imagined.

I felt the joy of discovery. The distances we had traveled became less real now at the end of the long journey. Now was the end of winter and the advent of spring. Here was a place to call home, a place to rest and restore and be sustained. I bowed my head and gave thanks.

To the men this resting place was good and rich and comfortable. To me, it was a reward and a tribute, and my heart wept in joy. The men understood but did not share my feelings about the journey. To them the movement was necessary and desired, a way of living. I traveled only because it was my calling. It was only when we reached each sacred place that the traveling seemed worthwhile and I could rejoice, the months of searching worth the long journey.

Each place we sojourned was more beautiful than the last, and the journey was, of course, nearer to its end than ever before. Still, I was tired. I longed for the time when the knowledge would be placed in the Earth so that we could stop the journey and finally return home. I wanted my time here to be done. The Earth and its sacredness were reflections of my true home, spirit, but it was not the same as home for me. The people said they could see the reflection of home upon my countenance and feel it in the quietness of my presence, but there were times when I did not feel it, so I kept silent and did not complain.

Never would I have them stop the journey on my behalf. I kept my own counsel, for it seemed to me that in every life we search for someone to understand completely the workings of our soul and yet we never truly find this. It seems impossible to communicate, for the very act of communicating changes the essence and makes it form, and the form alters the intent.

I longed for moments of true communication with each one of those I loved now, and those I had loved before—the communication which needs no words and comes more rarely than desired. And when that communication was not there, I kept my own counsel, the words unspoken, the longings held within.

Christ knew of this, and there were moments of this sharing where meaning was conveyed without the words and the knowledge was imparted through the pathways. Since our reunion he was even more present with me, and we shared our old intensity without the questions and the searchings. For as we had aged, we had seasoned, and our knowing was close to our hearts and minds, and this brought great joy.

I suppose I longed for Judas and Christ to be one so that I could experience both the spiritual and physical with one man. But Christ was not Judas, and even though I loved him, and the Mother had given us her sanction, it was not my place to be with him in the way of human merging. He was still Christ to me, and I knew my pattern and the design, and I lived it fully, trusting in the outcome I had seen. Yet there was an aloneness which came from seeing into all dimensions and knowing there was no one with whom I could share the experience physically.

Even as the others now followed me onto the golden field, joking and bantering, I knew they did not feel what I felt, and I knew they joked at times about me and the seriousness with which I lived my calling.

Our arrival was well timed. As with every spring, the Earth's crust was beginning to crack open, calling forth her resources from within, and the next day after we were settled, we performed a ritual, a ceremony to thank the Gods. We consecrated the Earth with our words and actions, pledging our intention to live in harmony with all nature spirits and with the elements and kingdoms who would come to help us. Through the ritual we awakened the fragrances and essences of beauty and brought them to bear on the Earth's surface.

443

The land was sacred, consecrated by the Gods to serve as a key to the memory of the inner kingdoms. Therefore, the land could be called upon to create conditions which did not exist in other places.

Since we had come as a part of the design, once we consecrated the ground by ritual, it would yield to us whatever we desired, whatever was the fulfillment of the highest potential of the design. Each aspect of nature knew this fulfillment, knew the pattern and how to best serve its accomplishment.
And so it was assured.

We planted and sowed seeds, harvesting crops to feed us for the next winter. We played and sang each day as a tribute to the land and the Gods and the growing plants which we nurtured. We were carefree, able to live as the people instead of as pilgrims bringing prophesy and knowledge. It was a holiday of sowing and mending and weaving, in preparation for the winter to come.

One day in the month of August, Christ approached me as I was weaving a basket, and sat down beside me. He loved to watch me weave, marveling at the speed with which my fingers worked the fibers. He watched me for a time and did not say words, sending me his accord as he sat. I knew he had something on his mind for he was very still. He smiled, but his smile did not touch his heart. Finally, he began.

"My Mary, it is time to prepare again for the journey."

I waited a moment before replying, tying off the end of the fiber and laying the work of the basket aside.

"I know," I said. "I have felt the chill beginning in the night, and the snows are asking us to seek lower ground."

He looked at me closely and began to speak again,
"My Mary, do you know where we are to go?"

I looked at him now just as closely and responded, "Yes, my love, we are to make our way to the place of your passing."

He did not hesitate. "Yes. It is time. We must leave the others now, you and I, and accord my turning."

It was one of the many moments when we came together and each held the other, knowing the design called us and that we must serve it. So we prepared to go. Our hearts were heavy, and we stayed close together through the days of our preparation, knowing the time was at hand.

After five months had passed, Christ and I were ready to leave. I loved this valley and honored the time we had spent. Christ and I said good-bye to the others of the calling, those who had chosen to travel with us and bring the knowledge to the Earth. They were new friends and followers, and this parting with them was the final one, for Christ and I were to go alone to his resting place. As we departed I looked back with longing, knowing I could never return.

And for me, in this life, there would be yet another leave-taking, the one from Christ. Then I would go alone to my final place of rest.

So I placed the vision of the golden grasses in my memory, knowing I would return there in my mind when I needed solace from the storms of my calling after he had died, and I was alone.

CHRIST'S PASSING

There are many levels of creation and many pathways of knowledge, and Christ had opened these during his ministry on Earth. When it came time for him to pass from form into light, the design was clear that the levels of consciousness he had opened on Earth were to be closed and remain closed until the light of Christ would return again to the Earth, 2000 years later.

When he died, the design he had carried would be placed into the Earth as knowledge and be held there by the kingdoms until the light of the people would come to free it. Christ had made the kingdoms one, and after his passing they would be held apart, waiting until the people remembered that they are the light, becoming one again with the Earth and her kingdoms.

Christ and I spoke of this in the ways of the world and in the ways of the Gods, and we agreed that I would stay behind to close the levels so that he could go: so it was he who went, and I who stayed. It was difficult for me and he knew this, for we were joined, and I did not want to be without him.

We spent the last few months of his life in constant sharing with each other and the ones with no names. He was the pivotal consciousness upon which the future was based, and what we were effecting would bear its fruits 2000 years from this moment.

We spoke of this, of the life we had together, of our love and of our calling, and we planned the time when we would again be together in the Swing between Worlds.

The day before we began the preparations for his passing, he came to me at dusk as the night pushed the day away, and sat down across from me. The air was sharp and cold, and we built a fire. He sat on one side of the fire and I sat on the other. He was pensive and yet determined to say to me what he had decided to say.

"My Mary, I must talk to you, for the words and the thoughts are crowding my mind, and there is no more room for them within me. Will you listen to what I must say?"

He was so grave that I felt suddenly chilled, but I knew there was nothing left to fear, for what we were facing was the end. We had done well, and now it was almost over.

So I inclined my head to him and said, "Of course I will listen to you, my love. It is my greatest pleasure to listen to you speak the words of your heart to me."

He rose from his place and came to sit beside me, placing his hand on my head and stroking my hair as he spoke.

"My Mary, I have been thinking of my life and the pathways we have traveled together, and I know that tomorrow we begin the ritual of my passing. I do not want to leave with these things unsaid."

He paused, gathering together the threads of what he would say.

"You know that you are the one most precious to me. I am grateful for your presence in my life, and for your steadfastness, and your forbearance. You have followed me and the design for all of your years, always facing the challenge and the calling, regardless of what the people have said of you. You have gathered great courage to your heart and gone forward, not knowing how, doing what, at times, seemed impossible.

I want you to know how much you have helped me and how much I am honoring you. I remember fondly all of the times that you taught me, gathering me to you and carrying me into the void, showing me the way home. Your union with truth has helped all of the people to know truth."

He stopped talking for a moment, his hand stilled in my hair, and he took a deep breath before speaking again. "I have known of your aloneness and your desire, and I wish again to merge with you as we did so many years ago after I learned of you and Judas."

He paused, and I wondered if he was turning the color of red again, as he had over sixty years before. We were old in the eyes of the people, and yet our bodies and our minds were keen and sharp and the flow of energy strong and fine.

I laughed out loud, and he held me, stroking my hair still, holding me ever closer. I understood that he had delivered for me my eulogy, for there would be no one to do so later.

451

He offered us both the chance to relive our union. And yet it was enough for me to be here with him now, the day before the preparations. I needed nothing more.

For I knew now that the union I had sought was within me and a part of us and had always been there. My restlessness lately had come from my knowledge of all time and my desire to live every part of my life in accordance with that knowledge. Because some of my people had not chosen to live in the same way, I had felt alone. But now, as the night came to sit between us, black and thick, I felt the comfort of the ages sitting there with us.

He felt these things within me, and we did not speak any more words except that I said, "Thank you, my Lord."

He held me, and we lay under thick cloths for warmth knowing tomorrow we would begin the preparations for his passing. We dreamed together in the flesh this one last time, remembering when, so long ago, we had lain as one in the way of the body. And there was no remorse and no longing, for we were one in the way of the calling, and we had found peace at the end of our long journey.

When we awoke, we began to prepare. It was ninety-nine days before his death, and there was much to make ready.

We took many layers of cloth and treated them with substances and essences, soaking them for thirty-three days.

We consecrated the ground with herbs and oils and set them afire, forging the substances into the Earth. The prepared cloths were laid on the scorched ground one at a time and were covered with tall grasses and branches woven to form a matted surface which compressed the oils and the cloths. The heat bonded the cloths and joined the essences within. These cloths remained thus for another thirty-three days.

During this time we began to prepare his body by closing the portals, or levels, in each point of transition. Attending solely to his body, he stayed grounded in the physical, keeping the pathways to spirit closed, and directing his consciousness into his cells. Then he unified with each cell, preparing it for the parting from form and the journey into light.

He bathed each day in water and then in oils, cleansing his cells and his skin. Purifying his system, he drank only water, and called the force of life from each cell to cleanse his body. When he had ordered his physical level, it was then time for him to open the gateway and begin his passing into the dimensions of light.

On the last day we placed cloths on the matted surface we had prepared and he lay down in his final resting place. I wrapped him in twelve layers of cloth, and when he was wrapped, I covered him with the remaining cloths that we had consecrated.

The period of transition was gradual and allowed for the Earth to adjust to the difference in frequency as his force of life was lifted out.

The actual parting of his body and soul took another thirty-three days. During this time there was a separating, level by level, cell by cell. Each level stratified before it left the physical. Moment by moment the form became less dense and more etheric, the spirit filling the cell and calling it home to being.

The density decreased and was reflected in the glimmering consciousness which had once housed his flesh. While the connection between the consciousness and the cells increased, the connection between the body and the cells decreased.

When his form was no longer needed it would dissolve, being absorbed by the awareness which had been the identity of the Christ.

I watched this process steadfastly, for its resolution depended on me. I tempered the levels, merging them through my knowledge, keeping constant communication with his soul. As the time came for him to pass, I held steady, praying to the ones with no names for the courage to let him go. I knew the design and the order. The levels were open to me, and so I was with them. And yet he was leaving and I was staying, and I felt the mortal pain of his passing. I was sustained by the knowing that he would stay with me in spirit until my own life was over.

When it was time, I lit three fires around him, and then I spoke to him out loud.

We had talked so much these last months that there were no more words, and yet I felt the need to speak, knowing it would release the tension and begin the movement.

He lay before me, the cloths of substance enveloping him, the fires burning around him, the night sky visible as a wave of blue flowing over the heavens pushing the day away. He could not see me now, for he was in the state of transition, and only the heart remained to beat with the human sound of living.

"I send you in light, my love," I said. "You have done well. I bear testimony for you and the love you have brought to this world."

I stopped. The tears formed a ball in my throat, and I swallowed so that I could begin again. I knew he heard my thoughts, and yet I needed to say the words aloud to make them real and to etch this moment in my mind and in my memory. For he had been a man of the people, and I felt the calling to honor him as they would through the speaking of his worth.

"All the days of my life have been graced by your presence. You are the light of the world, and I am grateful that we have been one in the calling. You have honored the truth of your light through all darkness, and I thank you. I will carry you in my heart always. I wish for you shalom, eternal shalom, for all time, and I release your spirit to the Gods."

There was then the beating of wings, and the humming was strong, and I led him, using the language of our oneness, and he followed.

g
n
i
s
i
r

His   light

and   his   body

f
a
l
l
i
n
g

And   as   he   died

time stopped

and   all   levels   accorded   him

There was a union

and

the sky and the land merged

becoming   a   w   o   l
                 a   f   i
                 v   g
                 e   h
                           t

which flew across the sky

FORMING A RAINBOW

and the Earth shuddered

and the sky

o   p   e   n   e   d

And the angels descended and lifted him as he died,

and all the Earth and her creatures sang in tribute to him.

And as I watched, I felt the calling of his soul through

all time.

And he was well rewarded, for he had accomplished his

design.

And then his spirit

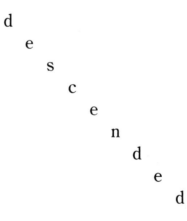

and for one moment

He stood before me,

the light of His being blinding my human eyes.

And within Him was the glory of the heavens.

And He surrounded me in this light,

in tribute and in acknowledgment.

I heard the voice I remembered saying,

"My Mary, my Mary, I love you, my Mary!"

And then He was gone

leaving a pathway of color and brightness upon the Earth.

The birds and animals gathered together around me then, and the sun and moon kept vigilance, lending their presence to the transition being created.

They knew the darkness was coming as the light left, and
they began to lend their sound in mourning and in
celebration. For it was both. The sadness and the joy
was felt together, for the ultimate result would be unity.
Through their acknowledgment they supported me,
and I gathered strength from them.

I stayed by his side for seven days. The animals lay near me to bear my
weight, and in those days I would drift into a weightlessness and join
with my departed one, spending the time in dreaming and in learning of
the transition. For I would need to create my own transitioning when the
time came for me to join him.

And when he had gone
the days were long, but the nights were longer,
for the body was old and the spirit fine;
and thus began the split of consciousness
so natural for a dying soul.

My heart was not wherever my body lay,
and I began to move as if in a trance-like state
of zealous questing
for the closure of energy in being,
to transcend the state of the human and evolve the
consciousness again fully into light.

And there came to pass a rendering,
and the Earth began its closure,
the days and nights being mixed,
and there was no separation.

As I walked, there were fogs of time and space
which emerged around me and caught me up,
so that I ceased to exist in any time,
and I was free to be, therefore, in all time.

My consciousness traveled in all dimensions,
and as I chose to leave the body,
my passageway to the knowledge of light
on the Earth began to diminish.

And the last portal closed as I walked the Earth.

THE END IS BLISS

The End Is Bliss

Jesus is Christ

In my dreams, Mary, I come to you.
Standing before you
I touch your hair and your face and your breasts,
and we are as one body
alive together through the dancing of cells.

In my dream there are no barriers and
we are one in the rejoicing.

The weave tightens—
the fabric of time and life,
and I cannot breathe.

The pulp of my blood and veins is squeezed
by the tide of death
which rides on the wave and comes forth around me.

I feel myself as the void—
with nothing—
surrounded by blackness,
losing my way,
finding not myself.

I gasp!
The breath held in my body
now released.

As my breath enters
I float,
my life and time
flowing before my sleeping eyes.

I see who I am as Jesus,
and who I will become
as Christ—
and I know it to be the plan.

And yet, what I see is my soul and my calling.
I see the light I carry,
and the future which will be,
because I have lived.

And I see my choices,
the many roads I have chosen to enter.

I see that they end in bliss,
the place of the soul's fulfilling.
And when I awake there are tears on my face
and contentment abiding in my heart.

And I think that when you awaken, Mary,
I will tell you what I have dreamed.
Tell you what I know!

That death is a dream
and life's end
but a sky
filled with starlit bliss.

MY PASSING

I stood on the mountain and I was truly alone,
for there was no one of my people
to send me to the other side.

And in that moment all became clear.
The vision I had sought was there with me finally,
as a part of my eyes, and a part of my mind,
and a part of my being.

I reviewed the events, for that was all they were. The
events of a time, and a place, and a soul, and a calling.

And in the end it did not matter, for the story could be rewritten many
times and in many ways, and the one God remained, and all the Gods in
attendance, and all the spirits and all the helpers. The angels and the
beings of light all remained, and did not stray from their watchful position
at the edge of time.

And as I stood
I was forgiven
and remembered
and chided
and teased
and judged,
and there was none of this,
all at the same time.

The cosmic perspective was one of gentle patience
and made the world's attention to detail and acquisition
a thing to be laughed at and dismissed.

I marveled at the design: the thoughts which create the
realities we all live and breathe, and which are upheld by
no condition of the universe.
How we truly create the realities we experience, and plan it
all so carefully to bring us to this moment of revelation.

And I smiled as I passed for I knew where I was going,
and the body was well contented with the end of this life
and the beginning of the journey into being.

I stood on the mountain
and this was the moment of my reckoning.
The moment when all that I had chosen was made known to me,
and the position of the soul was accorded,
and all was made real.
And all was remembered.

As I stood the realms began to merge,
and there was a resounding of all levels.
There was a calling which stirred me within,
gently making me aware of the truth of who I am:

> The daughter of time
> The woman of all ages
> The wife of the Gods
> The child of the people
> The wife and the lover
> The mother of all humans
> and all spirit.

All were one in that moment,
the roles merging
to bring me an identity
which transcended the need
of the human experience to define it.

I stood on the mountain
and my life force ran through my body and legs
into my feet which stood upon the Earth.
I listened with my feet as the Earth told me of her story
and showed me the lives which would come forth from this
moment.

I saw the images of my soul flowing from me as the blood
of my woman, sister, lover's blood.
And there was no separation between us.
All the souls I would inhabit in life experience, here on
this plane called Earth, were now visible, seen and
remembered, simultaneously.

And I followed and led at the same time,
seeing my lives played as truth before me,
open to scrutiny, and of course, to revision,
for I was in the creative moment, choosing as I left
how I would return, and when.

And I chose it in that moment and was born in another,
because they were the same.
I had the supreme knowledge of all dimensions
available to me, in this and all moments.

As I stood on the mountain
the Earth continued to teach me,
and I listened through the pores of my toes and my heels
and the arches in between, standing with my feet firmly
planted on her back.

And she was exultant!

For we had ended an era and were beginning another,
and all was for the purpose of the coming together of all
ages, as yet 2000 years in the future. . . Ah!

Future. . . Present. . . Past. . . . All now the same, in this
template of my knowing.
Yes, all the same.

The images of the people played before me:
those I had loved and those I had been scorned by, and those
I had scorned. And I knew that my destiny depended on
loving them and myself so totally that I remembered the bond
of the soul which made us one.

The truth of all time spun around me.
Faces merged into light
revolving around my consciousness.
I stood and drew the light unto me as a flame.

And as it drew closer
the world began to fade,
and with it all of the rules, the actions and reactions,
the grudges and the memories of separation, and I knew
I was going home.

I faced the mountains,
the mountains of Tibet,
sending out the call to all humans
and all kingdoms and all animals and elements
to guard the coming and going of all souls from this point
of reality so they would be guided into the truth easily. . .
could allow for the shifting of consciousness easily—
as a drop of rain merges again with the Earth in spring to
foster the growth of the green Earth,
dying, as each raindrop does, for the higher good.

And as I prepared to make my passage,
I felt the Earth take me in her arms and surround me.
Her love for me and her role as my nurturer changed.
We were friends and sisters first,
and I her daughter, and she my mother, second.

And I felt her rhythm then as I had not,
when choosing to live in the human way.

I felt her rhythm as a pulsing, orbiting frequency, tuned to
all other frequencies, terrestrial and non-terrestrial.
I realized fully her consciousness,
and saw what man would do to her.

I felt her forbearance and her tolerance,
felt her choice to love and to stay and to see it fully
through to the end, and into the years when the people would again
remember.

I vowed to her
in that moment of my passing
that I would always honor her and her essence completely.
And then of course, I saw the times when I would forget, and the
lives that would be necessary to teach me and to forge that
memory for all time.

I felt her forgiveness
and her knowing,
and knew that as I left this veil
and entered the courses of spirit,
I would take this consciousness with me.
I knew that aspects of myself would have different memories
and different challenges and would design the patterns
differently, and I sighed.

For there was no right or wrong, and she knew this.
She knew that the Hierarchy of Order had created a design of
perfection which would stand the test of all time, and all
souls, and all aspects.

I saw the ones who would follow me.
The ones who would carry the flame which was within my breast.
The ones who would carry the memory of truth into the faces
of destiny and fly apart and rejoin and die and be born, all
at the same moment.

And the thought I had as I closed the portals of earthly consciousness was that

   None of it mattered.
       And all of it mattered.

And in the letting go was the finding,

in the dying was the birthing,

in the destruction was the creation,

and it was all one, and we were all one, and all time was

     now.

    And the truth was alive in every soul
      in every time
      in every person
      and country
      and civilization
    and in every planetary system
      in all continuums
    through all time and space.

  T H E   T R U T H   W A S   A L I V E

The moments were merging, and there would come a time when
every aspect of every soul in every body would remember the
unity of all things, and there would be

Peace again on my mountain.

Peace again in my garden.

The wings were beating more loudly now,
the humming being stronger,
the noise of the passing, so familiar, now upon me.
And not this time for them,
for the ones I had helped to pass,
but for me.

I felt Him now clearly,
the part of myself,
the soul's male,
the one of the Christ.

And the merging began again—
                    the merging into being.

476

And we were flying now,
higher and higher
into the ethers of all seeing and complete being.

We flew over the Earth
and there was light,
and the light was the calling-forth of all souls.

I saw it,
and I knew that it was a gift from the Gods
showing me that I had done well.

In the end the design had been accomplished,
and I was shown its resolution.

And for the resolution, we were 2000 years from the moment
of this passing.

And the people joined hands across the seas,
their minds linked in one consciousness.
And there was no separation.
All children belonged to all people.
All marriages created union.
The death of competition became the birth of acceptance.
The greed was replaced with giving,
and the fear replaced with the memory of all kingdoms
dancing together in harmony.

And I watched the feet of the people
light upon the Earth.

They brought flowers
to celebrate their joining with
the Earth   the heavens   and each other.

For there was no separation.

They truly remembered.

And in that moment we were all one

and there was no time

and I died

and was re-born   and the memory was light

A N D   I   F L E W   H O M E

HOME AGAIN

Welcome Home!

All the lights awaited me,
their brilliance guiding me home.

I followed the light,
certain now of where I was.

What A Joy To Have You Home!

They formed a circle around me
their love coming to rest within me,
cleansing and soothing,
merging and resolving.

No longer human,
the lights gave me
a place with no form
and I settled there,
gratefully.

They drew me softly
into their presence,
blending their lights with
mine until we were
one light again.

They lifted me
and I rose as a
column of light,
spiraling into
the core of
creation.

EPILOGUE

IMAGINE!

Imagine all the players coming together.
The cast forming without conscious knowledge.

All the ties that bind bringing together the souls of time
to align once and for all, thus creating the most monumental
advancement in human consciousness ever experienced.

In all time,
                of all time,
                                for all time.

You are assembling now.
                                Now, you are assembling.

There is no way to move apart from the thrust of the import,
no way to negate the call, the call of the soul through time
                                for expression and resolution.

There are no borders within which to stay,
for the boundaries are moving faster than the resistance.

And for once,
the resistance has no form,
cannot carry with it the intention,
                                because none exists.

Imagine that now the players are assembling
to draw all together in the final act of humanity,

THE CHOICE OF HUMANITY FOR UNION.

Look and recognize our family, the family of our true origin,
for none other matters.
For it is only the family of your soul who calls.

Look only to the moment to bring you the joining you seek.
Look only to your soul to tell you the import of itself.

LISTEN! LISTEN TO THE VOICE OF THE

HARP AND THE DRUM!

L I S T E N

Listen! Time is calling. . . .

L O O K

Look! Time is hailing. . . .

Be with the hailing and the calling,
and deep within your self
you will feel the responding
rhythm of the beat of being.

Seek no further, for you have found the way home.

It lies within and has begun its last, true trumpet call.

You are assembling and therefore it is time.

There are no more questions to be answered.

Believe that this is the final act,

and the design is

truth in form

for all time

NOW

Edited by Jayn Adina and Noel McInnis
Book design, cover and paintings by Hannah Kleber
Photography by Flo Aeveia Magdalena
Typography by Kleber Graphic Design, Rockville MD
Printed in Canada by Webcom Limited

This book was typeset in Century Old Style and
printed on 60lb. Recycled Opaque, a 10% post consumer
waste and 50% post commercial waste recycled, acid-free paper.

Sunlight On Water
A Manual for Soul-full Living

Inspiration And Guidance For Our Time

If you have the thought,
the world is ready.
If you have the urgency, it's time.

By

The Ones With No Names

Received Through
Flo Aeveia Magdalena

Author of
I Remember Union

From

All Worlds Publishing

P.O. BOX 1462

NEW BRITAIN, CT 06050-1462

Phone & Fax: 860-832-9720

ISBN 1-880914-12-3

Retail $19.95 / 434 pages

Trade paper with illustrations

"We invite you to participate in this manual as a response,
rather than a reading. As a response, it will carry a charge.
Let the charge in, and it will validate for you
that you are a piece of Heaven...
and when you live that piece of Heaven absolutely,
Heaven can manifest on Earth.

Remember— There is a space for you in the world with your name on it...
and your part is the lead part. No matter who you are, it's the lead.
Because only you can play it, and without you it doesn't happen."

The Ones With No Names

FLO AEVEIA MAGDALENA & THE ONES WITH NO NAMES

- AWP BOOK & TAPE CATALOG -

Featured Selections

	ITEM	PRICE

I REMEMBER UNION - *The Story of Mary Magdalena* Paper, 1996, 496 pus.
The profound story of Christ and Magdalene and their legacy of peace for our
time. "The emotional side of Christ"...Ralph Bloom. "It will take your breath away."
NAPRA Review. "Another *Mists of Avalon...*" Karen Crane, *New Age Retailer.*

IRU $19.95

I REMEMBER UNION *"The Goddess"* on tape. Flo reads the poems and
passages of I REMEMBER UNION which focus on the growth and learning of Mary
as a priestess, Goddess, archetypal feminine counterpart of Christ. You will hear how
she assisted in the design of union and her part in the Christian legacy. 2 audio-
cassette tapes 1995.

#IT $19.95

SUNLIGHT ON WATER- *A Manual for Soul-full Living,* Paper 1996, 434 pus.
The Ones With No Names teach short-cuts for living fully and naturally from the soul
using exercises and meditations on how to hold the vibration of the soul in your
body and to connect from the soul in all of your relationships.

#SOW $19.95

✳ NEW TAPES FROM FLO AEVEIA MAGDALENA ✳
January, 2001

Living in the Hum—Align and Integrate the Four Levels
A Tape Series by Flo Aeveia Magdalena

Integrate mind, body, emotion, and spirit to bring order, peace and balance. Each side will feature an explanation
of the principles involved and a guided visualization. These will be appropriate for deeper meditation experiences
(Not to be used while driving!) You can order by the tape or set. Tapes are $12.50 plus $2.50 S&H or $15.00
per tape/$90.00 per set. (Set includes 6 tape case). Order number is #127S for series or #127-1, #127-2, #127-3,
etc. for individual tapes.

Tape One: The Order Matrix & The Four Level Meditation
Tape Two: Principles for Hearing Your Own Voice & Vibration
Tape Three: Opening & Balancing the Energy Centers
Tape Four: Earth Connection-Finding your Ground
Tape Five: The Twelve Power Center Meditation
Tape Six: Living in the Fluids of the Universe

✳TAPES FROM THE ONES WITH NO NAMES ✳
January, 2000

The Millennium and You
Many have asked us about the predications of upcoming changes that abound
concerning the new millennium. The Ones give sound guidance as to how to view the
changes, prepare for what is to come, and use this time as a vehicle for
putting our wisdom to use.

#125 $12.50

The Six Steps to Mastery Series

Tape One: Breath and Light
Tape Two: Cellular Vibration and Memory
Tape Three: Circuits and Pathways of Energy
Tape Four: Non-Reactivity and Freedom
Tape Five: Heart First and Compassion
Tape Six: Choice and Intention~Ways to Surf the Wave

Beginning in August The Ones channeled a tape per month on the six steps to mastery. These tapes include exercises and the intention for each tape, each month, to build the vibration and awareness to incorporate the choice for mastery based on the pathway from the previous tape. Each tape is $12.50 plus $2.50 postage and handling.	#126	$69.95

If you order the set for $69.95 plus $10.00 shipping and handling, you save a total of $10.00.

Transcripts of **The Millennium and You** and **The Six Steps to Mastery** are now available. $70.00 for Mastery Series (in a loose leaf binder) and/or $12.50 per tape transcription.

The List

SEXUAL FULFILLMENT:*Ways To Express The Yearning For Union* from the forthcoming book RE-SOLUTION: *The Fluid Way to Harmony in Living*. Booklet with exercises which prepare all the bodies for physical intimacy.	#sexful	$8.00
VIBRATIONAL HEALING SOUNDS 1990. This tape of healing sounds and tones assists you to move energy through your body and to feel the cellular design of the divinity within by re-patterning the energy fields around the physical, mental, and emotional levels, bringing harmony and relaxation.	#101	$12.50
UNION: THE MARRIAGE OF MALE AND FEMALE 1990. Understand the energy dynamics of relationship and how to create an environment where union can be felt in your most intimate life experiences.	#102	$12.50
THE FIRST TWO YEARS: *Helping Your Child Adjust* 1990. Instruction on birthing and raising children during the first 24 months, the crucial time when their connection to the universe is most available. Hear what to do to support and assist them to maintain their connection to the source.	#103	$12.50
AIDS: THE MESSENGER AND THE MESSAGE 1992. Side 1. Aids as a consciousness raising aspect in human evolution. **GROUNDING** Side 2. Bringing the body and spirit together. The principles and specifics of being in the body, fully alive, and connected to the earth.	#104	$12.50
THE 1990's - LIVE YOUR POTENTIAL! 1992. Side 1. NOW is the time to bring your destiny & potential into the moment and live your essence more completely. Learn how to bring forth your part of the design. Side 2. How the 90's are different from any other time in history for the fulfillment of your destiny and the design of humanness. Shift your perceptive and live the promise now!	#105	$12.50

THE MODEL OF COOPERATION 1991. Specific instruction in the upcoming model for society based on resource sharing, universal awareness, and cooperation. Principles include ways to live in reception from the universe as we put in our part of the design. Truly a model we can get our hands on! Changes our conscious money practices! Edited version is in *Sunlight On Water*.	tape- #106 transcript-#107	$12.50 $7.50
THE BRIDGE OF LIGHT 1991. We are in a time called *The Coming Together of the Ages*, the time of the remembering. The wisdom of all time is now available to us, and our choices now affect how this knowledge will manifest on our planet and how our reality will be shaped. An inspirational channeling about our capacity to co-create societal models of peace and harmony in the next twenty years. Edited version is in *Sunlight On Water*.	2 tapes-#108 transcript-#109	$14.00 $12.50
HOLOGRAPHIC LIVING 1992. This tape explains concepts such as parallel reality, systems theory, and how to manifest from substance using holographic principles. Covers both personal & professional models, telling how to utilize these universal principles to create and to see & feel yourself as a part of the whole.	#110	$12.50
THE NAMELESS ONES DICTIONARY OF TERMS 1994. A definition of terms and concepts used by The Ones With No Names in their messages and channelings. (This is included in Sunlight On Water.)	#111	$14.95
CHANNELING AT MASONITE SPRINGS CONFERENCE 1994. Learn to smooth your edges, creating union with those who push your buttons! A fun tape about using every experience in your life to create union.	#112	$14.00
GUIDELINES FOR SOUL RECOGNITION FACILITATORS *from The Ones With No Names*, December 6, 1995. What is the soul and how is Soul Recognition a necessary part in creating the next step for our species?	2 tapes-SRFTAM	$12.50
LAST CHANNELING OF TOWNN, DEC. 6, 1995 The last public channeling which took place in Unity Church, Gaithersburg, MD. The free will experiment was over on December 31, 1995. How do we create through divinity instead of karma, and live the design of union in our daily lives?	2 tapes-#113	$12.50
DEC. 28-31, 1996 THE LAST CONFERENCE OF TOWNN Held in Lewes, DE, this series takes us through unifying our energy fields; the mind, body, emotion connection; programming our life from the design; entering the holographic envelope; living with a "soft mind"; how the design works; re-patterning our cellular body; accessing our part of the hologram and much more.	9 tapes-#114	$100.00

TAPES RECORDED IN 1998

UNION OF THE 12 UNIVERSES: *The Purpose of the Heaven on Earth Community.* What are we really doing in Vermont? What role do we play in the greater design. How does the physical space hold the design of union for the planet.	#115	$12.50

THE TIMES OF RENDERING: There will be 5 major times of rendering between now and 2005—times when old realities and paradigms no longer create our life experience and we must choose to live in union from soul and to seed the future <u>in the future dimension</u>. How do we best move through these times with choice and strength, and how do we create and seed our heart's intention into the future?   #116 $12.50

RAISING CHILDREN: *Guiding Masters.* There are 3 stages in a child's development and unfolding—ages 0-7; 7-14; and 14-21. Learn to guide your child's mastery and be aware through these times of growth and foundationing.   #117 $12.50

AUTHENTIC RELATIONSHIPS: *Creating the third Point.* Remove your masks, live in commitment to authentic relationship with yourself and your life partner, creating a third point of union instead of co-dependence.   #118 $12.50

FAMILY SYSTEMS: *The First System of Union.* We choose our birth family of origin as a group of souls with whom to experience and learn union. We can foster union both with our original nuclear family, and with our current family, the nu family of our children. The concept that we have chosen these souls to learn abc union changes many of our human dynamics.   #119 $12.50

CLARIFYING YOUR LIFE'S PURPOSE Live what makes you happy, in the moment, with direction, allowing the action and resolution to be created from the energy of your connection with creation. When we begin to connect more fully with the wave of our creation, our purpose manifests automatically.   #120 $12.50

THE WAY HOME: Being here fully as spirit in form requires bringing the essence of our divinity into our body and being physically present and balanced in our male and female. Living creatively with the presence of the Sophia, the energy which fosters the sourcing and richness of human life, brings us to deep peace about being here on Earth.   #121 $12.50

ALTERNATIVE EDUCATION FOR ATTENTION ALLY DIFFERENT CHILDREN (ADD) How to honor each child's needs and create learning environments where children participate actively in their education, establish a group structure to bring balance and accountability, and begin to draw forth and live their essence and presence.   #122 $12.50

HOW TO MANIFEST: Create the foundation for your visions in the world and begin to ground them into form. A fun, how-to tape which brings the desire and the connection into place to facilitate manifesting what is in your heart.   #123 $12.50

HUMAN DYNAMICS: Hear about the underlying dynamics which exist between people and learn to create resolution and understanding as you relate with others.   #124 $12.50

All Worlds Publishing Book & Tape Order Form Jan 2001

MAIL TO: All Worlds Publishing
P.O. Box 1462
New Britain, CT 06050-1462   USA
Phone & Fax 860-832-9720

Send to:

Name_____   Address_____

City_____   State_____   Zip_____

Phone   (home) _____   (work)_____   fax_____

Email   _____

Please send the
following items:

Quantity	Item Number	Price

Add $6.00 S & H for each book USA/$10.00 Foreign

Add $2.50 S & H for the first tape

and $1.00 for each additional item

Total

Mastercard or Visa   Number   _____   Exp. date_____

Signature   _____

(Add $2.00 service charge if using credit card)
Make check or money order payable to "All Worlds Publishing"